RON PAUL

FATHER OF THE TEA PARTY

Jason Rink
VARIANT PRESS

Visit our website at www.variantpress.com

Edited by Bradley A. Porter
Cover designed by Hayden Sundmark
Printed in Canada

Library and Archives Canada Cataloguing in Publication

Rink, Jason, 1974-
Ron Paul : father of the Tea Party / written by Jason Rink.

Includes index.
ISBN 978-0-9868322-1-5

1. Paul, Ron, 1935-. 2. United States. Congress. House--Biography. 3. Legislators--United States--Biography. 4. Presidential candidates--United States--Biography. 5. Tea Party movement-United States. I. Title.

E901.1.P38R56 2011 328.73'092

C2011-905724-7

This is an unofficial biography. Ron Paul and anyone related to Ron Paul do not sponsor, authorize or endorse this book.

Acknowledgements

We would like to thank the following people for their research and contributions to this book: David Bardallis, Trevor Bothwell, Tom Eddlem, Benjamin Fenton, Rick Fisk, James Herndon, Chris Horner, J. H. Huebert, Kyle Jones, Johnny Kramer, Karen Kwiatkowski, Lucas Mafaldo, Stephanie Murphy, Geoff Pike, Lasse Pitkamieni, Bradley A. Porter, Joshua Snyder, John Suarez, and Vedran Vuk.

Contents

Chapter 1

Sitting in the green room at CNN in early 2007, Ron Paul waits patiently as his makeup is being refreshed for another interview. He had done two that morning—each a short ride from the other—and had an hour to kill until his next. Since forming an exploratory committee in January, getting television time had been a challenge, so Paul, at the behest of his small staff, had adopted a policy of not turning down a venue, no matter how hostile. The interviews he had done earlier that morning played to a now-familiar script. Lacking any more material on Rudy Giuliani or Hillary Clinton, producers turned to the also-runs to fill airtime. Invariably, that entailed introducing Paul, letting the viewers know what a long shot he was (always—always—they referred to his campaign as "quixotic"), and then segueing into a discussion of his "radical" views. During one of his earlier interviews, the anchor had immediately begun reading from a list of Paul's positions with a growing, theatrical air of disbelief. "You want to abolish the Department of Education? You would do away with the FDA? You want to end the War on Drugs? You want to return to the *gold standard*?" And, as with every interview, Paul waited patiently to make the same core philosophical argument while the interviewer baited him and clearly delighted in painting him as a crank.

In those early months of the 2008 presidential campaign, Paul differed from the other candidates in that he was just as likely to receive boos from Republican audiences as he was to be cheered—assuming he could manage to get an audience at all. And, the next day, he had to go out there and do it all over again.

Sitting in a hair and makeup chair with a paper bib around his neck, a producer pops in to let him know they will be ready for him in 15 minutes. The makeup artist finishes and leaves, and Paul is, once again, left alone with his thoughts. The son of a dairy farmer in Pennsylvania, a small-town doctor used to delivering babies in Southeast Texas, here he is counting down the minutes until he gets the privilege of getting called crazy on TV. He's as committed to the message as ever, but he can't help wondering, again…how did he get here?

Getting off the boat at Ellis Island, a 14-year-old German boy named Caspar had likely wondered the same thing as he clasped his father's hand and followed the dirty, exhausted crowd off the gang-plank. The boy is Ron Paul's grandfather. A year earlier, Germany had abandoned the silver standard, causing the international value of precious metals to plummet and throwing the major economies of Europe into a tailspin. This became known as the Panic of 1873, and Capsar's father, like so many, found himself in the middle of economic chaos. Deciding that Europe no longer held the kind of opportunity he wanted for his son, Caspar's father joined hundreds of thousands of other Europeans in making the perilous journey across the Atlantic Ocean. His son in tow, he traveled from Schlüchtern, a small town in the Hesse state of the German Empire, to the United States of America.

The pair landed in New York and made their way to rural Pennsylvania, which they knew held a large population of the Pennsylvanian Dutch, many from their home region of Germany. The small town in which they eventually settled shared a congenial similarity to Schlüchtern, so they decided to stay. But the trip had taken its toll on Caspar's father, and shortly after their arrival he passed away. Young Caspar suddenly found himself alone, in a foreign country, left to fend for himself.

There was no Child Protective Services agency to put Caspar into foster care. There were instead orphanages, charitable organizations, and churches, all of which helped him cope with the loss of his father. There was a small federal immigration agency, but Caspar was in no danger that it would deport him back to Germany, so he remained in America, as his father had intended. And there were no child labor laws to prevent the teenager from earning a living, so he set about trying to do just that. He was undoubtedly heartbroken, poor, lonely, and scared, but he was free. So, with a resolve he knew his father would have approved of, Caspar moved to the nearby town of Green Tree Pennsylvania, and set out to make a living.

Farming was all Caspar knew from his old homeland, so it was agriculture that he was immediately drawn to. In particular, a new market had opened up that was called truck farming. It involved growing fruit or vegetable crops on a large scale, and then transporting them to sell in other regions where unsuitable climates limited their production. He found he had a knack for recognizing where markets were inefficient—areas where customers demanded produce, but where supply had not moved to meet them. So he began to set about exploiting those inefficiencies. In the winters, when he couldn't grow crops, he added a dairy to his operation, selling milk and eggs from his basement.

As he built a respectable business, he was also active in the community, and a regular churchgoer. It was at church that he met a striking young woman named Sophia Ziegler. Although Sophia was born American and raised in Pennsylvania, her parents Johann and Gertrude were also from the Hesse state in Germany—whereas Caspar had arrived fleeing turmoil, Sophia's ancestors had arrived seeking it. During the American Revolution, thousands of Hessian soldiers were contracted as mercenaries to fight against the colonial rebels. Ironically, these immigrants of Hessian descent were now enjoying the society that some of their forebears had attempted to crush.

Sophia and Caspar married on May 4, 1899. They had four sons: Herbert, Howard Caspar (born August 19, 1904), Louis, and Arthur; and one daughter named Estella.

Caspar Paul, after enduring hardships unimaginable to many, had finally created the life that his father had wished for him.

By the 1920s, Caspar and Sophie were advancing in years, and they decided it was time to pass the family business—now flourishing—to their children.

Herbert, the oldest, didn't want to work in the family dairy. Instead, the budding entrepreneur opened up his own Agway store, part of a chain of stores selling farm supplies. Estella, the only child to get a college education, set out to become a teacher. This left Howard (the second oldest), Louis, and Arthur to inherit the family dairy and farm land. They expanded the basement dairy their father had started into home delivery, initially using horse-drawn delivery wagons. As their business grew and technology advanced, they eventually came to own a modern dairy and twenty refrigerated trucks.

During the tumultuous time of the Great Depression, the Paul brothers began families and continued to operate their dairy. On October 23, 1929, twenty-five-year-old Howard married a young woman named Margaret "Peggy" Dumont. They had met in a social group called Luther League, part of the Lutheran church they both attended. Peggy's parents, Joseph and Lena, were both locals born in Pennsylvania. Peggy eventually became the bookkeeper for the Paul brothers' dairy. Surrounded by family and with a thriving business, Peggy and Howard were happy, and ready for children.

Ronald Ernest Paul was born on Tuesday, August 20, 1935, the third of what would be five sons born to Howard and Peggy in the Depression-era thirties. Ron joined older brothers Howard William "Bill" and David Alan, and an extended family at the Green Tree,

Pennsylvania dairy farm. This included his paternal uncles, Louis and Arthur, and grandmother Sophia. The family would soon be complete with the births of younger brothers Jerrold Dumont and Wayne Arthur.

The extended Paul family, and all five boys, worked hard from an early age, busy with school and church. Years later, Ron's wife of fifty years observed that his was not "a family that played a lot. Everything was serious."

Howard and Peggy Paul were active Lutherans, and Howard hoped that all of his sons would grow up to be Lutheran ministers. In fact, two of his sons would join the clergy—Ron's older brother David later became a Lutheran minister, in Michigan, and his younger brother Jerrold became a Presbyterian minister in New York. Ron recalls that he briefly considered becoming a Lutheran minister, but eventually decided on a different path of service.

As a child, the Paul family emphasized church, work and study—in a community that valued the same. Ron recalls that "what influenced me most in my family and upbringing ... was the work ethic and church. It was faith-based. We spent a lot of time at our church and that was part of our routine."

Ron's earliest memories included happily sharing his room with his brothers. His brother David recalls they "grew up in a house with five boys in one bedroom." In 1940, five-year-old Ron received his first paid job working alongside his brothers in the basement of their four bedroom house. They were tasked with checking hand-washed milk bottles for spots, earning a penny for every dirty bottle they identified coming down a conveyor belt.

Howard and "Peggy" Paul posing with their children

"We learned the incentive system," Ron recalls. The recycled bottles were washed by Ron's uncles, and one uncle was a little more careless than the other in this duty. "We liked to work for that one uncle, because we got more pennies."

Ron was halfway through his first year in school when news came of the Japanese attack on Pearl Harbor, and the US entry into the Second World War.

In 1942, Roosevelt established the War Production Board, the Office of Price Administration and other government bodies to oversee federally mandated production goals, and price controls throughout the economy, including the important agricultural sector. So began the wartime economy in the United States, complete with government rationing of food and commodities, as well as edicts and required approvals for a wide variety of human enterprises that only months before had operated freely.

While the Panic of 1873 was the defining economic event of Caspar Paul's early life, for young Ron it was World War II. He observed his father duly affixing a government issued sticker to his car windshield, with authorization numbers to match his government issued ration tickets for gasoline. He observed his mother checking her ration book with its stamps for the family's various food and sundry needs. Because the Pauls ran a dairy, delivering milk, butter and cheese directly to local customers, the onerous hand of the nationally managed economy reached into the Paul household on a daily basis, in an unprecedented manner. In addition to government concern over the production of dairy products by small farmers, rationing placed a new government burden on all retailers, who were required to collect the stamps for rationed items from every customer.

Although Ron was too young to begin forming concrete political beliefs, the events around him were shaping his values. Those values centered not on forced sacrifice, a common value around wartime, but on freedom. "I claim that I was born with it," he later recalled. "I think a lot of us are born with instincts that we'd like to be left alone in our privacy, and my instincts were there. I think I was conditioned over the years by our educational system and what our government tells us … that you're a strange person because you believe that."

At the very least, he had one escape from worry about war, money, or government edicts: sports. The athletic teenager was an avid baseball player—later in life one of his favorite childhood stories was that Hall of Fame shortstop Honus Wagner was on his milk route. And, lithe and in good shape from his farm work, he found he could distinguish himself in games with local boys by his speed around the bases. He became such a speed threat that he began developing a new passion—track.

"Ronnie" Paul posing for his school photograph

Before Ron Paul would ever run for political office—before he would ever find himself sitting alone in a makeup chair waiting for his minute and a half of air time—he would run simply for the joy of it.

Chapter 2

In the fall of 1949, fourteen-year-old Ron Paul entered his freshman year at Dormont High School in Pittsburgh, Pennsylvania. Known to his classmates as Ronnie, he distinguished himself early as a top athlete and a diligent, friendly student. His peers even persuaded him to run for president of the student council. The shy Paul had to be talked into it, but once he agreed, he was easily elected to his first political office.

Throughout his four years in high school, Paul excelled due in no small part to the work ethic conditioned in him from his years at the dairy. In fact, he continued to work at the family dairy throughout high school, and he added to that a job at the local drugstore. By the time he became a sophomore, he was an honor student, spent dozens of hours working at the dairy, dozens more working the register at the store, and piled on top of that a full week's worth of practices and games in at least four different sports.

He was on the football, baseball, and wrestling teams but, perhaps owing to his individualistic streak, it was track and field where he found the most success.

As a sophomore, he placed second in the state in the 440-yard dash. In his junior year, he was the Pennsylvania State Champion in the 220 and 440-yard dash and placed third in the 100-yard dash. Paul's time in the 100 was 9.7 seconds, which was just shy of the national record at the time – "pretty fast for the early 1950s," his future wife, Carol, remarked.

As he began to acquire a national reputation for his track success, including offers of college scholarship, he suffered a serious knee injury while playing football.

Paul joining the track team

Paul was almost always outsized by his opponents on the field, but he was quick and nimble and possessed a certain fearlessness that served him well. High school football was popular in Western Pennsylvania, and his team entered the field to the sounds of his fellow classmates, family, friends, and neighbors, cheering from the stands. Paul—well-liked and known for his speed on the field—received a particularly pitched cheer.

He sat on the sidelines, lacing up his mud-spotted cleats, watching his team's defensive unit take on the opposition, and anticipating his chance to jump in and move the ball towards the end zone. When it was finally time for the offensive line to take over, he threw on his plastic helmet and took to the field. During the next play, his quickness failed him and he went down. As one defenseman after another piled on, his knee was hyper extended. The crowd grew silent, and coaches and teammates surrounded him. Paul sat in the grass at the 40-yard-line, his hands on his knee, wincing in terrible pain. And in that moment, his future as a competitive track star flickered out.

The injury required surgery to repair a torn ligament, and months on crutches. After rehabilitation, although he was able to walk again, his knee was no longer the same—it felt wobbly and weaker than before, a condition that would plague him throughout his adult life. In time, he painfully came to accept that his competitive track days were over, although he never stopped running.

A few good things came out of his knee injury. He was required to undergo extensive swimming therapy in high school as part of a rehabilitation program. As with everything he did, he threw himself into that too, and soon took up competitive swimming. And he also gained a deep appreciation for the medical profession.

Back in school, Paul was an enthusiastic learner, and one of his favorite subjects was history. With it, he gained a tremendous respect for his history teacher. Unfortunately, the Korean War raged almost entirely during his high school years, and in his second year his history teacher was drafted. The year after, he was killed in action. It was a formative learning experience for the young student.

As he later recalled, "Clear memories of the horrors of World War II and the Korean War and the reports of loss of life of family, friends, and neighbors had an impact on me. I knew very early on I never wanted to carry a gun in a war…I definitely knew at an early age that I preferred a medical bag to a gun, healing to maiming, life to death."

Paul's class of '53 yearbook entry

Throughout the remainder of his high school days, Paul accumulated several scholastic and athletic achievements, and even took to the stage for a school play *Young April* based on the 1926 film of the same name. But it was his personality that most people noticed. Even as a youngster, he had about him a quiet magnetism that impressed classmates and teachers alike. He was humble yet confident, a true believer in the adage that in order to gain respect you must first give it.

It was the sum of Paul's character and personality that drew the attention of a beautiful schoolmate, Carol Wells. Carol was from nearby Dormont, another borough just outside Pittsburgh, adjacent to Paul's native Green Tree. She was the only child of Bill Wells, a successful coffee broker, and Carol Wells Sr. Even as a young girl, Carol was the type of person who made everyone with whom she came into contact feel respected.

Paul first caught Carol's eye at a high school track event, but she knew him from school as well. "I think what impressed me most was that everybody liked him," she recalls. He was also something of a boy scout—a serious student and athlete, and not, in her words, part of the "dating crowd", or otherwise prone to mischief. That posed a bit of a problem for Carol. Paul was so preoccupied with studies and sports, it might be awhile before he ever noticed the pretty sophomore waiting to be asked out. As she turned 16, she took matters into her own hands. At the upcoming Sadie Hawkins dance, where the girls invite the boys, she invited Ronnie. Afterwards, the pair went steady for the rest of their high school days.

Paul graduated with honors in 1953, and was also voted "best all-around" by his graduating class. With his high school education drawing to a close, he was about to embark on his life's journey.

Yearbook cartoon

Chapter 3

Early in life, Ron Paul contemplated the idea that he might become a Lutheran minister—the same career chosen by his brothers David and Jerrold. However, the Korean War and the death of his history teacher had a life-altering impact on him. He decided on a path that would grant him entry into medical school.

After graduating from high school in 1953, Paul matriculated to Gettysburg College, 200 miles east of his hometown of Green Tree, Pennsylvania. He had turned down track scholarships at other schools, including Penn State, because he felt that his knee injury—although rehabilitated enough for schools to still be interested—would prevent him from performing at a high enough level to justify taking the money. Besides, Gettysburg was small, church-oriented, and he had a good friend who was a sophomore there. It was a good fit.

While Paul was at Gettysburg, Carol still had another year of high school to complete. Fortunately, she could stand outside the school, look up a hill, and see her family's modest two-story house about five blocks away. If she saw that her mother had hung a towel outside, it was her signal that a letter from Paul had arrived.

After Carol graduated from Dormont High, she attended Ohio University in rural Athens, Ohio. There, she majored in secretarial studies and home economics, and was a marching-band baton twirler and a member of Alpha Xi Delta, a self-described "women's fraternity" founded in 1893. Every day during those college years, just as she did during high school, she sent Paul a letter.

He read her letters—along with mountains of textbooks. One classmate remembers of him that he was "usually seen either going to the library, or coming back to the fraternity house with an arm load of books."

Enrolling at Gettysburg College

Paul's athletic career continued at Gettysburg, as he joined the swim team and continued to run track and field, although with more difficulty than in the past. He joined the Lambda Chi Alpha fraternity, which bore the distinction of being the first national fraternity to publicly take a stand against hazing. Gettysburg was also a dry campus, and Lamda Chi Alpha employed a housemother who enforced the rule. Thus, while the popular perception of fraternities of the era is dominated by the raunchy movie *Animal House*, Lambda Chi Alpha offered something different at Gettysburg—and that's what attracted Paul. "Every fraternity has a different reputation—some were only sports, some were only playboy types, but Lambda Chi was well-known for academics and having a lot of well-rounded people in a lot of different activities as well as sports. The fact that they represented all the different areas and cared about having good grades, I thought it would be better because I wasn't into the drinking and the things some fraternities were known for." As Carol had gleaned during high school, Paul was as straight-laced as they came.

From the outset, he was a leader in his fraternity—first, as president of his pledge class, and later as the chapter secretary. Additionally, he became the group's house manager, a job that paid $9.00 a month. He later added "kitchen steward" to this list. He recalls, "You had to order all the food, plan all the meals; you were in charge of the cooks for three meals a day, seven days a week. I got $43 a month for that and that paid for my food... and the food was good because I got to buy it."

Among Paul's closest friends in the fraternity were Richard Lewandowski and J. Michael Bishop, a fellow biology student who would go on to win the Nobel Prize in 1989 for his research on viruses that can cause cancer. When Paul wasn't busy with his many activities, he enjoyed relaxing around the fraternity house. A pool table provided a favorite form of indoor recreation for the group.

Future Nobel Prize winner J. Michael Bishop

In the fraternity house and around the campus, Paul's character was evident to all who came in contact with him. Mrs. Lewandowski recalls that he was not only pleasant and polite, but also an obviously "honorable man." She also notes that he blended sociability with honesty. "If you asked his opinion on something," she recalled, "you would know he was telling you exactly what he really thinks."

During his adolescence, he had earned and saved enough money working at the dairy, mowing lawns, delivering papers, and working at his regular job at the drugstore to pay for his first year's tuition—$325 plus expenses. The fraternity job paid his rent, and he had a small academic scholarship.

He also delivered laundry part-time, and in his second year he became the manager of "The Bullet Hole," a campus coffee shop (named after the Gettysburg College athletics teams, the Bullets).

On Christmas breaks, back in Green Tree, he delivered mail as a temporary mail carrier for the US Postal Service. (As a Congressman and presidential candidate decades later, he would support eliminating the Postal Service's monopoly on first-class mail delivery and call for competition.) During summer breaks from college, he delivered milk for his father's business, Green Tree Dairy, filling in for regular drivers who had gone on their summer vacations. All these jobs allowed him to pay his college tuition, put aside money for medical school, and purchase a special—and costly—item that forever changed his life.

Despite their separation during college, Ron and Carol stayed in touch. They both sent daily letters through the post office, and they saw each other whenever they could. She would sometimes go to Gettysburg to watch him run track or visit him for his fraternity house party weekend. Other times, Paul went to Athens, Ohio to escort Carol at her sorority dances.

In the summer before his senior year, the two went on a picnic in Dormont Park near their families' homes. The park's swimming pool was a major center of social activity for young people in the area. On Independence Day, townspeople sat on a small hill overlooking the pool to watch fireworks launched from the pool's parking lot.

At a picnic on July 20, 1956, Ron made some fireworks of his own on that hill by proposing to Carol. She wasn't surprised by the proposal because they had talked about marriage. But she was surprised by one thing: she thought she would have to wait until after Paul's college graduation before they could afford a ring. Instead, Carol recalls, "I got a lovely diamond." Then and there, his habit of saving his extra earnings suddenly paid off.

During a break between semesters in his senior year of college, Ron and Carol were married. The wedding ceremony was held on

Friday, February 1, 1957, at 7:30 p.m. at the Dormont Presbyterian Church, and attended by more than 300 guests. Snow covered the ground outside making for a spectacular white wedding.

At the reception's end, guests knee-deep in snow tossed rice as the married couple crouched into their car and headed off to Durham, North Carolina. The growing city not only served as the location of their honeymoon, but it also gave Paul an opportunity to visit Duke Medical School. The newlyweds had a chance to see the town in which they might soon live. "We decided we liked it," said Carol. Ron applied immediately so that he could begin studying there the next fall.

Celebrating with the happy couple

Before medical school would begin, there was a final semester to finish at Gettysburg. Paul moved out of the fraternity house and into a third-floor apartment of an old Victorian house in town on Carlyle Street with Carol—a move made possible by his extra jobs. Their apartment couldn't be accessed from inside the house. Instead, they had to take a spiral staircase outside the house up to their new home. They fastened some bells to a rubber band so that visitors could tug the band from the ground below to let the Pauls know they were there.

Immediately inside the apartment door, there was a living room to the left and a kitchen to the right, with the apartment's only bathroom next to the kitchen. Carol recalls that if someone were undressed in the bathroom when visitors arrived, this could create a rather difficult situation, as the unclothed individual had no means of escape.

The house was just down the street from the Majestic Theater. It was a movie theater then, but Ron and Carol didn't go often. "We aren't big movie people," says Carol. (More than 50 years later, Paul would return to the same theater during his 2008 presidential campaign, where he gave his own "Gettysburg Address" before more than 800 enthusiastic supporters.)

With the rent at $50 per month, Carol worked through the rest of the school year as a secretary in the registrar's office and also typed papers for professors.

Living in Gettysburg, the Pauls could go anywhere in town by walking. If they needed to travel some distance—say, to Pittsburgh—they had a gift from Carol's grandfather Wells for that: a 1949 Cadillac.

The Pauls knew this was a rare period in their lives. Carol recalls that they "wanted to make time for each other because we knew it would be more difficult when he started medical school." Paul had a light class schedule, and therefore had more spare time than usual.

Some 51 years later, Carol recalled these few months at Gettysburg as a "fun-filled time" in the couple's life together and a "great beginning."

On May 19, 1957, Paul graduated from his final year of college. He was destined to enter medical school, after which he could fulfill his dream of becoming a physician. The young couple could scarcely predict the excitement which lay in their future as they embarked on their journey together.

Chapter 4

Ron Paul had applied to the Duke University School of Medicine while finishing his bachelor's degree in biology at Gettysburg College. His exceptional grades at Gettysburg aided in his acceptance, but it was his half-hour interview with the dean that impressed the administration with his commitment to becoming a medical doctor. He was accepted and matriculated at Duke in 1957.

Paul and his newlywed wife Carol headed to Durham, North Carolina where they would make their new home. Carol soon found work as a medical secretary. They rented a tiny blue frame house that Carol's grandmother nicknamed "the doll house," due to its quaint dimensions. After settling into their new home they purchased a furry brown and white female collie to live in their spacious backyard.

Life in the doll house

By 1957, the Duke University School of Medicine was among the top five in the country. Duke's medical school (like Duke University) was research-oriented. Traditionally, medical students learned the basic medical sciences in their first two years, followed by clinical rotations in their third and fourth years. At Duke, Paul would receive one compressed year of basic sciences, followed by clinical rotations in the second year. This allowed for a third year of medical research, where he would take on a small research project.

Paul's first year at Duke was not much different from his college years. Much of his time was spent taking copious notes as a professor lectured in front of the class and wrote on the chalkboard occasionally. There were also many labs, where students did everything from producing viral cultures to dissecting cadavers.

Attending Duke University

The second year took Paul much closer to his ultimate goal of becoming a physician as he and his classmates learned how to diagnose patients. During clinical rotations, they visited hospitals and interviewed patients under the watchful eye of a doctor, who provided guidance and confirmed the students' diagnoses. The students would even analyze blood and tissue samples in an attempt to arrive at a proper diagnosis. It was an exciting time for Paul, who was, for the first time, doing the work of a medical practitioner.

During his second year of medical school, the couple's first two children, Ronald ("Ronnie") and Lori, were born at Duke University Hospital, in 1958 and 1959 respectively. According to Carol, their well tempered collie helped raise their first two children. The dog even made a financial contribution to the family one Thanksgiving by giving birth to a litter of puppies. The young couple was able to sell one of the puppies for thirty-five dollars, which gave them enough travel money to drive home so that their extended family could meet their two new infants.

While in medical school, Paul developed a passion for politics and economics. It was ignited by Boris Pasternak's *Dr. Zhivago*, a gift from his mother Margaret. The book made a case for the threat that government bureaucracies pose to creativity and liberty.

It was at this time that Paul's interest in economics and politics expanded even further, perhaps as a result of applying his diagnostic approach to the body politic. Like a true doctor, he focused on curing the underlying disease rather than just the symptoms. Despite his exhausting workload and his responsibilities as a husband and father, he remained a voracious reader.

He would later reflect, "Early on and during the '60s as a resident I liked to read things other than just medicine. I became fascinated with economic policy and came across a school of economics called Austrian Economics. It is a free market, sound money type of economics. It's a little different than just saying conservative economics because they believe you can't have paper money but have sound money. It also deals with limited government."

One person who influenced Paul philosophically was Leonard Read, who established The Foundation for Economic Education (FEE). According to Paul, "He was a very lone wolf after WWII. Everything had become big government and internationalist. He wrote a lot of articles himself and revived some classic articles that were forgotten, like Frédéric Bastiat's *The Law*."

A profound influence of Paul would be the Austrian School's greatest proponent of the early twentieth century, Ludwig von Mises, who has been hailed as "the first great modern critic of Socialism." He famously said, "Economics deals with society's fundamental problems; it concerns everyone and belongs to all. It is the main and proper study of every citizen."

During Paul's fourth year at Duke, the medical school focused on preparing students for their work as physicians. They had sufficiently developed their diagnostic skills that they would debate different treatments and why they favored one over another.

The responsibilities of parenthood combined with the discipline of medicine meant that Paul was used to operating under pressure. He would not only survive, but thrive in that high stress environment, traits which suited both a medical doctor and a future political leader.

Paul received his Doctor of Medicine degree from the Duke University Medical School in 1961. It was a thrilling graduation. He now had his M.D., but he did not yet have a license to practice medicine. For that, he would have to complete one year as an intern at a hospital.

Paul was just becoming aware of the problems of government interventionism in his chosen field when he set out to find a hospital willing to accept him with his freshly-minted medical degree. His grades and personable attitude ensured he would find a good hospital. He was immediately accepted at the Henry Ford Hospital in Detroit, which offered one of the nation's oldest and most respected training programs for new doctors. Henry Ford Hospital had, by then, taken its place as a major urban hospital, with more than 500 beds on a 20 acre site, more than 20 operating rooms, a 35,000 volume medical library, and a new 17 storey clinic building. It would be a challenging and fruitful place to learn the practice of medicine.

The couple loaded up their 1949 Cadillac and drove almost 700 miles along the Interstate 77 with their two small children, Ronny and Lori, and their collie. They arrived in Detroit, which was at the height of its prosperity, twelve hours later.

The Henry Ford Hospital was founded as a philanthropic project in 1915 by the pioneering industrialist whose name it bears, at a time when the great American capitalist was a staunch opponent of America's entry into the First World War. It was a fitting place for the future leading voice of pro-market non-interventionism to begin his medical career.

Interning at Henry Ford Hospital

In the early 1960s, a 100 hour or more workweek was normal for interns, spent under the supervision of senior doctors. Fortunately, medical interns were paid, unlike interns in some other professions. Paul received a salary of $195 per month.

Carol ran a dance school from the basement of their home to supplement their income. From this home studio, she taught ballet, tap dancing, and even occasionally baton twirling. The income that Mrs. Paul brought in with her private dance lessons was vital given the modest pay her husband earned as an intern. Years later, Carol recalled, "Just to tell you what kind of a budget we were on, the dancing school paid for the newspaper and for extra expenses we had."

At Duke, Paul had learned the breadth and scope of medical knowledge that had been accumulated since the days of Hippocrates, the "father of medicine" from Ancient Greece. At Henry Ford, he put his knowledge to practice. He received hands-on training in internal medicine, that branch of the medical arts specializing in the diagnosis and treatment of diseases, especially those of the internal organs. Called internists (not to be confused with interns), practitioners of internal medicine are often called "the doctor's doctor," as they are called upon to have an encyclopedic knowledge of the many ailments and maladies that strike the human body. The internist is trained to see and treat the body as a whole, to tackle enigmatic diagnostic problems with an analytical and holistic approach, often having to handle both chronic diseases and the occurrence of multiple ailments at the same time. It was this approach that Paul would later bring to his diagnosis of the political and economic ailments afflicting America.

Paul's keen eye was focused not just on the human body and the many things that can go wrong with it. He observed his hospital's organic functioning within the society to which it belonged. He later recalled, "The amazing thing was it was a city hospital and there was no government; there [was] very little insurance and nobody was turned away whether they were illegal or legal, and nobody, nobody was quizzed. If you didn't have the money, you didn't pay, and people came in, and it wasn't that bad. People didn't lay on the sidewalks. You're more likely to hear stories today of people being neglected in emergency rooms—and dying on stretchers—because we have managed care."

This awareness led Paul to that towering enemy of collectivism in all its forms, Ayn Rand. An émigré from the nascent Soviet Union, Rand described herself as a "radical for capitalism." As one of the twentieth century's most influential and controversial philosophers, Rand reached an enormous audience primarily through her works of fiction, her two most famous novels being *The Fountainhead* (1943) and *Atlas Shrugged* (1957). Both books were poorly reviewed but became runaway bestsellers. A 1991 Library of Congress and the Book-of-the-Month Club survey ranked the latter as the second most influential book after the Bible.

Rand had around her an inner circle of intellectuals that included Alan Greenspan, an economist and part-time jazz musician. Ironically, he would one day become Paul's chief nemesis as

Chairman of the Federal Reserve.

Paul later said of Rand's books, "Nobody gave her a review, and anybody who did said it was horrible, horrible, horrible. It was word of mouth and she still sold millions and millions of copies because she was telling the truth and people were anxious to hear it."

Despite being immersed in the study of medicine, and his recreational study of politics and economics, world events also grabbed the attention of the 26-year-old husband and father at the beginning of an exciting and promising career in medicine. The first year of his residency saw the erection of the Berlin Wall and a year later the Cuban Missile Crisis would put the world on the brink of nuclear annihilation. These two years also saw the quiet escalation of American involvement in Vietnam under President John F. Kennedy.

They were troubled times, yet they would bring happy news to the Paul family. As Paul was nearing the end of his internship, he received news that Carol was expecting the couple's third child. In January 1962, Carol bore him a son, Randal Howard Paul, who would forever bear the mark of this fertile period of his father's intellectual development; a son they would later call "Rand".

Chapter 5

In the late fall of 1962, a twenty-seven year old Ron Paul was nearing completion of his internship at the Henry Ford Hospital in Detroit, Michigan. Once finished, he hoped to continue with his residency where he would practice medicine. His anticipation was tempered by the knowledge that once he and his fellow interns completed their internship, they might be drafted into the Army.

The United States was squaring off with the USSR in the buildup to the Cuban Missile Crisis. Years later, Paul recalled, "I got the draft notice during the [October 1962] missile crisis. The draft notice said, 'You're going to be drafted and you're going to be sent into the Army unless you want to volunteer. If you volunteer, you can be a captain, you can practice medicine and you can join the Air Force.' I immediately volunteered." Soon, he was commissioned an Air Force First Lieutenant.

The Paul family—four-year-old Ronnie, three-year-old Lori, and newborn Randall in tow—soon hit the road, bound for Kelly Air Force Base (AFB) outside San Antonio, Texas.

As lifelong Pennsylvanians, Ron and Carol were unprepared for the fine weather and wide-open spaces of south-central Texas—and they loved it. The family settled into a rented house, and Paul began service as a medical officer at Kelly AFB, the Air Force's oldest continually active airfield. Only a few years earlier, the B-58 Hustler, the United States' first supersonic bomber, was entered into the inventory. Maintenance responsibilities for this aircraft, as well as F-100 and F-5 fighter aircraft, were assigned to the Kelly Air Force logistics depot. In 1960, the 433rd Airlift Wing (the "Alamo Wing") was activated from a reserve unit and moved from nearby Brooks AFB to Kelly AFB. Four years later, the Alamo Wing would become the first Air Reserve unit to win the coveted Air Force Outstanding Unit Award. Lt. Paul was assigned to the 433rd Medical Group as a flight surgeon, responsible for the medical treatment and certification of pilots, aircrew members, and air traffic controllers.

Exposure to pilots and aircrews, their stories and experiences, and flying with aircrews and medical personnel to various locations inspired Lt. Paul to pursue his private pilot's license. He earned that license during his first year at Kelly AFB, and often flew young Ronnie and Lori in a small plane around the area. Carol also flew with him—once. Ron and Carol also joined a bowling league of doctors, dentists and pilots, and splurged on his and her bowling balls.

First Lieutenant Paul in the US Air Force

Life in Texas was good, with Lt. Paul making $700 a month, significantly more than he had made during his residency at Henry Ford. Even with the increased income and discounted military shopping at the base commissary and exchange, Paul filled in several evenings a week at a local church hospital emergency room for $3.00 an hour. For the Pauls, working hard and working several jobs was normal.

Carol had helped to put Paul through medical school, and the young family was used to frugality. In Texas, for the first time, she didn't have to work for a supplemental or even the sole paycheck. She remembered this interval at Kelly AFB as a time of plenty, where they saved and were able to replace things that they needed, in the expectation of dire finances when Paul pursued his medical specialty after his term of active duty. It was during this time that Carol first learned the art of cake decorating from a pilot's wife in San Antonio. Years later, she would teach a cake decorating class at Ohio University and author the locally-famous *Ron Paul Family Cookbook* series.

Life for the Pauls was lively, happy, and—in Carol's words—"so much fun" in San Antonio between 1963 and 1965. But while their personal lives were full of joy, the military, at the time, was constantly on edge. Years earlier, while Paul was treating patients and working overtime as an intern at a Detroit hospital, the 1961 Bay of Pigs invasion had been launched, and had publicly failed. Havana, as a Soviet-sponsored communist capital in the Western hemisphere, was at best a political thorn in the side of Washington and, at worst, a flamboyant sign that communism was indeed encroaching. The Cold War was heating up.

Just months before Paul entered the Air Force, the United States and the American military had participated in an alarming showdown with the Soviet Union over the possibility of Soviet mid-range nuclear warheads stationed off the coast of Florida. If the 1962 Cuban Missile Crisis set the tone for national security thinking before Paul's enlistment, American military interventions abroad provided the texture of his time on active duty.

In 1963, when Paul joined the Air Force, there were about 16,000 Americans deployed to Vietnam. By 1965, when then-Captain Paul left the active Air Force to serve three more years in the Air National Guard, that number had grown more than ten times to over 184,000. Air Force transport, fighter and bomber pilots were increasingly affected by and serving in Vietnam.

The early 1960s also saw US military interventions, including military air transport operations, in the Congo (then Zaire) and Guatemala. The strengthening of NATO against the Soviet threat in Europe and the expansion of the Vietnam conflict were occurring—even as the first post-World War II-era military aircraft and weapons were rolling off American production lines, employing many of Paul's neighbors, co-workers, and both military and civilian patients in the San Antonio area.

Lt. Paul's duties as an Air Force flight surgeon in 1963 and 1964 involved certifying Air Force pilots for flight status. He met a number of pilots deploying to the Vietnam theater in the early 1960s, as well as some returning from Southeast Asia. When he signed the medical paperwork for these skilled pilots to go into the battle zone, he increasingly thought about what they were doing there, and why.

His assigned medical specialty was treating the ear, nose and throat problems of pilots and aircrew, and he was also called upon to assist in the investigation of several aircraft accidents during his time on active duty. "I recall doing a lot of physicals on Army warrant officers who wanted to become helicopter pilots and go to Vietnam," he recalls. "They were gung-ho. I've often thought about how many of those people never came back."

These flight surgeon duties took him far from Texas. In fact, he traveled to over twenty countries during his active-duty service, which took him to East Asia, Europe, Latin America, and the Middle East, although never to Vietnam.

At the time, each of these countries was allied with the United States. They stood as bulwarks against communism. In years to come, self-determination movements, conflicts with their neighbors, and domestic political movements would test and challenge the very definition of words like freedom, communism and anti-communism, and the credibility of policymakers in Washington, DC.

In late 1963 and early 1964, Paul became involved with the presidential campaign of Senator Barry Goldwater, a small-government Republican known for his strident and bold anti-communism. There was also an Air Force connection, as Goldwater had been promoted to the rank of Major General in the Air Force Reserve in 1962.

Goldwater was expected to face off against President Kennedy in the upcoming election. Paul met Kennedy on November 21, 1963, in San Antonio. The President was in town to dedicate the opening of the new Aerospace Medical Center at nearby Brooks AFB. The next day he was assassinated and Lyndon B. Johnson assumed the mantle of president.

At the time, Paul observed both those running and affected by foreign wars, as well as the Cold War-driven growth that shaped modern San Antonio. His up-close exposure to the fascinating 1964 presidential campaign and the libertarian Old Right perspectives of Senator Goldwater was complimentary to his Air Force role and duties.

Although Goldwater was against foreign wars, Democrat Lyndon B. Johnson in his infamous "Daisy" commercial insinuated that Goldwater would start a nuclear war. He also ran ads claiming Goldwater was associated with the Ku Klux Klan due to his opposition of the Civil Rights Act of 1964. In truth, the libertarian Goldwater was opposed to the federal infringements on state and individual rights in the act. Johnson easily won the election in 1964. Despite that disappointment, Paul's association with Senator Goldwater was important in helping to refine his views towards the constitutional role of the federal government and the framework of a constitutional foreign policy for the United States.

Looking back on those formative years, Paul said, "I was in the US Air Force in 1965, and I remember well when President Johnson announced a troop surge in Vietnam to hasten victory. That war went on for another decade, and by the time we finally got out 60,000 Americans had died. God knows we should have gotten out ten years earlier."

Decades later, Paul noted that after US withdrawal, Vietnam became a friendly nation committed to capitalist ideas. He contrasted this history to the US history of economic and political warfare with Cuba, and the utter failure of America's Cuban policy to promote freedom for Cubans or to eliminate a possible threat to US national security. He understood the true nature of the foreign policy of interventionism that America had pursued for over a century. Non-interventionism and free trade were more effective than war.

Paul's experiences—as a flight surgeon, as a commissioned Air Force officer in that critical time of the early 1960s, as a witness to the mistakes of one American interventionist and idealistic president after another—convinced him of the clear and constitutional logic of a foreign policy of non-intervention, and the social, economic and security benefits of freely trading with all countries, while allying with none.

By mid-1965 America was entering into a new era: the Civil Rights movement was at fever pitch with demonstrations throughout the South, prompting Johnson to propose and sign into law the Voting Rights Act, a monumental step towards civil and political equality. Coincidentally, the government was facing criticism for the escalation in Vietnam, with which a vocal segment of the population disagreed. It seemed as though a political and social revolution was capturing the American spirit.

Other revolutions were occurring as well, even in the medical community. By the time Paul would finish his residency, the first human-to-human heart transplant had been performed and the birth control pill was experiencing widespread use.

It was during this age of change that Paul chose his career. Before volunteering for the Air Force, he received a year of basic medical training as an intern. Now he would continue his training as a resident physician. His grueling residency, filled with 80-hour work weeks, would allow him to learn and practice medicine under the watchful eye of experienced senior physicians.

Previously he was planning to complete his residency in internal medicine. However, after two-and-a-half years as an active duty officer, he began to favor obstetrics, the surgical specialty dealing with pregnancy. In July 1965, he transferred to the Pennsylvania Air National Guard in Pittsburgh. There he would complete his residency in obstetrics and gynecology at Magee Women's Hospital. His progress would be monitored and administered through the University of Pittsburgh.

In Pittsburgh, Ron and Carol were able to rent a house that was near both their parents' homes and directly adjacent to the house of Carol's aunt and uncle, Bob and Lois Clark. The relatives had a swimming pool in their backyard that the kids enjoyed. This came in handy as vacation time for Paul was scarce. The close proximity of their extended family was also important because Carol was three months pregnant at the time, and it always helped to have family nearby when someone was needed to look after their three young children.

The couple began attending St. Paul's Episcopal Church in Pittsburgh, as all of their children had been baptized Episcopalians. Paul's family was Lutheran, and Carol's family was Presbyterian, so they were familiar with all three churches in the area.

By December of 1965, Carol was overdue in her pregnancy with the Pauls' fourth child. Because of the heavy snowfall at the time, he was worried that the couple might be snowed-in and unable to get to the hospital before natural birth, and so on December 21, 1965, Robert Alan Paul was born by induction.

Paul continued to meet his monthly requirements with the Air National Guard, even while focusing on his residency. He was on night-call every other weeknight and every weekend. As a result, short visits with his young family were the only times he could truly relax.

Aside from his newfound interest in economics, another experience also greatly shaped his future political thinking, and would in large measure inform his thinking on one of the 20th century's most hot button issues. All physicians until the 1970s were required to take the Hippocratic Oath before practicing medicine, in which they promise to do no deliberate harm. Paul took his oath seriously, and, having shown a special interest in obstetrics/gynecology, that included the lives of his unborn patients. Before his residency, he had no familiarity with the process of disposing of the unborn. "The issue never came up. I never heard the word abortion," he later recalled.

Late in his residency, as he was doing rounds at Pittsburgh Medical Center, he was called into an operating room where a hysterotomy abortion was being performed on a patient who was seven-months into her pregnancy. The procedure is similar to a caesarian section, only requiring a smaller incision. At that time abortions were illegal in the State of Pennsylvania, but many doctors still routinely performed them and thought prospective physicians should be trained in the procedure (as a matter of practice, residents were not required to participate if they objected). Paul was called in to observe the procedure, so he obliged.

As he tells the story, near the end of the procedure he saw the doctors lift out of the mother a fetus that weighed approximately two-and-a-half pounds. He heard the baby gasp for air and begin to cry. As the child was screaming and squirming, the doctors placed the fragile infant into a bucket which was placed in the corner of the room. Paul's face turned flush with what felt like shame, though he didn't say a word. He uncomfortably stole glances at his fellow doctors, wondering if they saw what he saw. He stood dumbfounded as everyone in the room acted as though the screams of the baby didn't exist. After a few short minutes, the screaming ceased. He walked out of the operating room a changed man.

To him, it seemed like the physicians were ignoring the Hippocratic Oath, which was still fresh in his mind. As he would later write in his 1983 work *Abortion and Liberty*, "All of my medical training was directed towards saving life and preserving health."

After witnessing an abortion first hand, it was clear to him that the procedure ran counter to those values—it was, in his words, a "barbaric act." For the rest of his medical career, he refused to perform or witness the procedure again, and vowed to fight for the sanctity of life, wherever that fight would lead him.

Paul valued innocent life due in no small part to his experiences as a father. In Pittsburgh, while his children were growing up in front of his eyes, he decided to pursue a career of obstetrics/gynecology as a practicing physician. And he would respect his Hippocratic Oath in the only way he knew. He vowed, "I will maintain the utmost respect for human life, from the time of its conception."

Chapter 6

Near the end of Ron Paul's medical residency in Pittsburgh, Pennsylvania in 1968, he was performing surgery with a colleague and chatting, as doctors often do. The Soviets were gearing up to invade Czechoslovakia, which was in the midst of democratic reforms. Eventually the topic of conversation turned to Paul's post-residency plans.

Ron and Carol had both enjoyed living in Texas during his service at Kelly Air Force Base. They had planned to return to San Antonio where Paul had even been offered a position at the University of Texas Health Science Center, a new medical school which would open its doors in 1968.

Paul's colleague had a different suggestion. The only practicing obstetrician/gynecologist (OB/GYN) in Brazoria County, Texas, was leaving his practice for personal reasons. The practice was in Lake Jackson, a small town approximately fifty miles south of Houston and ten miles upstream from the mouth of the Brazos River on the Texas gulf coast. The doctor there was looking for someone to take over his practice.

Paul thought carefully about the costs and benefits of each career path, and later admitted that he was "torn between academic medicine and going into private practice." He decided he should go to Lake Jackson to meet the doctor who was stepping down.

The Lake Jackson practice was a modern, one-story building. The physician there had recently invested approximately five thousand dollars in a hydraulic table—new technology at the time. He was eager to leave right away. As Paul remembers, "he essentially gave me the practice." Paul agreed to pay off the balance of debt on the hydraulic table, and collect the remainder of the other doctor's receivables, which Paul then mailed to him at his new address. He would also inherit the practice's staff. After they made their agreement, the transition was rapid. As Paul put it, "I arrived July 4th, and he left the morning of July 5th."

Carol arrived in Lake Jackson with their (now four) young children and (now two) collie dogs. They were, in Carol's words, "ready to start on a wonderful new life in a town that was full of churches and friendly people."

Carol was slightly hesitant to leave their home in Pittsburgh. She was, however, persuaded by Paul's reassurance that if she was unhappy living in Lake Jackson after one year, they could go someplace else. She quickly grew to love the small, rural town. In contrast to the cities of Detroit and Pittsburgh, where they had lived in the past, Lake Jackson was warm and sparsely populated. It was an excellent place to raise children, with many parks and baseball fields.

In the late 1960s, the corner of southeast Texas known as Brazoria County was an area dominated by agriculture, albeit not far from the major cities of Houston and San Antonio. More than two thirds of the county's land at that time was considered prime for production of such staples as rice, corn, and dairy—in fact, cattle outnumbered people. The land was dotted with farms, businesses and, of course, the sprawling Dow Chemical plant.

The Dow site covered more than three thousand acres, and was the original impetus for Lake Jackson's existence. The junction of the Brazos River with the Gulf of Mexico also provided a port and accompanying harbor about ten miles downstream from Lake Jackson, which were occupied by shrimp boats and container ships.

With the population growth in Brazoria County during the late 1960s came an increasing demand for obstetrical care. As Paul had predicted, his services were much needed. During his first day in practice, his office was filled with what he later estimated to be thirty women. He was soon delivering up to fifty babies each month. "Within a few months," he said half-jokingly, "I was struggling to get a day off."

Dr. Paul working in his medical practice

He recalled that in the early days of his practice, there were no pagers or cell phones to let him know that he was needed at the hospital. Instead, if he was out on a weekend enjoying a little league game with his family, a police car would pull up to the baseball field and let him know that a call was coming in. But despite the busy lifestyle that accompanied his practice, he was satisfied knowing that he was providing care to a medically underserved community. "They needed him so badly here," said Carol.

At Paul's office, there were no frills or fancy decorations, but it was always kept neat and clean. A small sign out front read, "Ronald E. Paul, M.D." The office reflected Paul's tendency to shy away from anything ostentatious. It was clear that the focus of his practice rested solely on his patients.

Paul's patients were as diverse as the population of Brazoria County itself. They ranged from the affluent to the indigent, and represented a wide variety of ages. Most patients had health insurance through private providers. Some who did not carry medical insurance paid for their care out-of-pocket; a few were eligible for Medicaid or Medicare. The majority of Brazoria County's inhabitants in the late 1960s and early 1970s were Caucasian. However, a significant portion of the women there were Black and Hispanic (predominantly Mexican).

Some physicians in southeast Texas at the time were reluctant to care for poor women from racial and ethnic minorities who often could not pay for their care. Even Medicaid reimbursements were too low or too cumbersome to obtain. By contrast, these women were welcomed at Paul's office—even if the government payments were not. He quickly gained a reputation for helping those who had no money. Indeed, he believed in the moral responsibility of physicians to care for everyone, regardless of their ability to pay. He never worried about the financial impact of treating indigent women for free in his practice. In his words, when women came to him seeking his help, he "just took care of them."

Most of his patients who were short on funds would one day pull themselves out of their situation and remain loyal patients. The foundation of this business model rested on his belief in caring for the needy through voluntary means, as opposed to government intervention.

From the outset, Paul never accepted payments from Medicare or Medicaid. He dealt with private insurers, and also accepted out-of-pocket payments. If he knew that a patient was stretched financially, he allowed flexibility on the price, even sometimes bartering with patients for goods rather than accepting cash. According to Dr. Jack Pruett, Paul's partner in the medical practice, "He never even sent a bill" to poor patients who would have relied on Medicare or Medicaid at other physicians' offices. The practice was busy, successful, and lucrative—so much so, in fact, that he could easily afford to treat needy patients for free and still thrive.

As a result of his commitment to his patients and quality of care, he was popular and well-liked within the community. He believed in honesty with his patients above all else. If a medical error occurred, which it rarely did, he would immediately explain to the patient what happened, and he would apologize. It was clear to his patients that Paul took his relationship with them seriously. As a result, no lawsuits were ever brought against him—a rarity in the field of medicine, even at the time. In fact, Paul never carried malpractice insurance.

As a result of his expanding clientele, the first several years of Paul's Lake Jackson practice had been, as he described it, a bit "overwhelming." He had been considering adding a practice partner for some time.

Paul first met his practice partner, Jack Pruett, in 1974. Pruett had just finished his medical residency at Scott and White Memorial Hospital in Temple, Texas. Paul called the director of Pruett's OB/GYN residency program, and asked if there was anyone he could recommend. Pruett's name came up immediately.

As Pruett recalls, "When I walked into his office, the first thing he said to me was that there were two things that he and I had to agree upon or else there was no use for us to even talk. He said, 'Number one is, we do not do any abortions.'" Paul had decided, due to experiences during his residency in Pittsburgh, that abortions were simply something he could not in good conscience perform. Pruett expressed his agreement, and encouraged Paul to continue. "He said, 'Number two is, we also do not accept any federal funds. We are going to see Medicare and Medicaid patients for free, and we are going to treat them just like we treat everybody else regardless of what it costs us to do that.'"

Pruett was unsure about the idea of refusing federal funds at first, but he decided to give it a try. He immediately hit it off with Paul. And for twenty years thereafter, they conducted their practice on nothing more than their word and a handshake, without a written contract of any kind.

Their initial agreement was that Paul would pay Pruett a salary for six months. If both were satisfied after that time had elapsed, they would become full partners. Pruett was impressed by the trust that this agreement showed; it was unusual for a practicing doctor to add a full partner in such a short amount of time. But, after half a year had elapsed, both physicians were happy to enter into the partnership. Paul saw patients in the office on Mondays and Wednesdays; Pruett saw patients on Tuesdays and Thursdays. Whichever of them was not at the office would be at the hospital delivering babies and taking care of their patients. On Fridays, both did double duty, covering the hospital and the office as needed.

Because of that arrangement, the patients had access to at least one doctor who would be available twenty-four hours a day, seven days a week. Both physicians were seeing all of the patients, so they each took an equal share of any income that the practice generated.

Paul worked tirelessly. He was often on call, delivering babies in the middle of the night. But he was as fastidious about caring for himself as he was for his patients. He ate a healthy diet, never smoked, and ran, swam, or rode his bike diligently every day.

However, as the years went by, medical malpractice became an increasingly pressing issue—not for anything happening in their practice, which had a spotless record, but due to changes in the field of medicine and medical insurance. In the 1970s in Texas, the legal concept of Joint and Several Liability allowed damages from any suit successfully brought against a doctor to be collected from an affiliated hospital, if the hospital were found to share any portion of the liability. Administrators at the Community Hospital of Brazosport were well aware of the risk this presented to them, especially from areas of medicine with intrinsically high complication rates such as obstetrics. The administrators announced that they would require all affiliated physicians to purchase malpractice insurance, and that anyone who refused to do so would be fired and replaced with someone who would purchase insurance. The high cost of malpractice insurance can be a significant factor in driving up costs for patients, and even deterring doctors from practicing in certain fields where premiums are high.

Drs. Paul and Pruett "saw the writing on the wall," and called a special meeting with the other area physicians who were also affiliated with the hospital. Nearly all of them pledged that they would not purchase malpractice insurance. The plan was to leverage the collective bargaining power of many physicians against the hospital in order to defeat the new requirement. However, a few weeks later, Drs. Paul and Pruett found out from hospital administrators that they were indeed the only ones who had not purchased insurance. Dr. Paul's office, it turned out—despite the others agreeing in principle—was the lone "no" vote.

This was an illustrative example of how most doctors in the early 1970s behaved. They took their jobs seriously, and all they wanted was to practice medicine. But when it came to politics, or activism of any kind, few besides Paul deviated from the status quo.

There were other examples of Paul's increasingly political nature. He and Pruett worked with the Brazosport Birthing Center, a small area facility that employed approximately five nurse-midwives. In his perpetual willingness to take a principled stance, he was an outspoken proponent of midwifery.

He also took every opportunity to publicize the fact that he did not accept government funds at his practice. He and Pruett spoke at county medical board meetings and other gatherings of physicians in the area, as well as individually with local doctors, explaining their business model. In principle, most local physicians agreed with him in his consistent refusal to accept government money. However, in their own practices they faced pressures to accept government intervention in medicine in the form of Medicare, Medicaid, and all of the accompanying mandates and red tape. When faced with powerful institutions such as the American Medical Association and Texas Medical Board, all but Drs. Paul and Pruett quietly fell in line.

The Health Maintenance Act passed through congress in 1973, ushering in a new age of government managed healthcare. Paul described managed care as "a general nuisance," noting that it dampened his efficiency as a physician.

Delivering babies at Brazosport Hospital

He found that managed care undermined his clinical judgment. For instance, HMOs placed time limits on office visits, refused to pay for procedures if the patient did not fit a specific profile, and refused to pay for the newest drugs, which were sometimes a better choice for the patient than older, less expensive ones. For Paul, this was the common thread between Medicare/Medicaid and HMOs: they undermined the doctor-patient relationship. He believed that it was the doctor's job to decide—with the patient—the best treatment on a case-by-case basis, synthesizing all kinds of information to make the best determination. HMOs, on the other hand, used "one size fits all" formulas, sometimes created by non-MDs. Paul believed that these could never replace the personalized decision making of a physician who knew his patient.

He referred to the new system as the "Medical-Industrial Complex," a parallel institution to the infamous Military-Industrial Complex. "We have developed a Medical-Industrial Complex because government runs medicine," he explained. "We have corporate medicine; we don't have free market medicine."

Despite his disagreements with government and HMOs, Paul had become a popular member of his community almost immediately after he first began practicing in Lake Jackson. Anyone who knew a baby recently born in Brazoria County also knew Doctor Paul. He was well-respected by other area physicians, and had a reputation for keeping current with all of the latest medical journals. Above all else, it was his compassion that won over the hearts of those in the community.

Pruett recalls a time in the early days of his partnership when they cared for a young Mexican woman. She and her husband, who worked in Galveston at an offshore oil refinery, had three small children. She did not have health insurance, so she paid out-of-pocket for her prenatal care. Drs. Paul and Pruett had been caring for her all through her most recent pregnancy with triplets.

When she reached approximately eight months gestation (an unusual occurrence, because women pregnant with triplets are at high risk for preterm labor and birth), they had instructed her to rest in bed until it was time for her to deliver her babies. In the past, she had always placed a lot of trust in the doctors, and had followed their medical instructions carefully. But one day, they received a call from her saying that she had to go to Galveston because her husband had suddenly become very ill. Pruett gave her the number of the nearest emergency room, and told her to go to that hospital if she started to have any contractions. She did make it back from Galveston before giving birth, but unfortunately, her husband did not survive his illness.

When Drs. Paul and Pruett found out what had happened,

they refunded 100% of the money that she had paid for her previous medical care, and delivered her triplets at no cost to her. After the babies were born, they arranged for local businesses and large companies to donate formula, diapers, and baby clothes. With six children at home and her husband gone, she was unable to continue to support herself alone in the United States, and so she ultimately returned to her family in Mexico. But for years, Drs. Paul and Pruett received her Christmas cards. She even sent them a handmade ashtray as a gift to express her gratitude for what they had done. Paul cherished the ashtray, though neither doctor smoked.

The overwhelming feeling Paul had during his initial years practicing medicine in Lake Jackson was affection. As Carol put it, "He just loved medicine; he loved delivering babies. Any other doctor can make you well, but the obstetrician actually gives you a present. And the present of new life is so special."

But as Paul opined in a 1996 interview, "When your job is to bring new life into the world, it makes you really aware of what kind of a world these children are coming into, and what they have to face." He wanted to make sure they could lead happy, free lives and to have a hopeful future.

Although his medical practice had been deeply rewarding, his dissatisfaction with the nation's political climate had been steadily growing since the inception of his practice in 1968. Rampant inflation and mismanagement of the country's currency, price controls, and increasing government regulation of every aspect of Americans' lives were some of the issues that plagued his life. When President Richard Nixon announced that he was severing all remaining ties between gold and the dollar in 1971, Paul felt he could no longer remain a spectator.

Just as he had held fast to his principles in medicine, he felt that he could no longer keep quiet about what he saw as an out-of-control government in Washington, DC. It was time for him to begin a new chapter in his life.

Chapter 7

Studying economics as an intern had painted an unsettling picture of America for a young Ron Paul. Now that he was 39, he more fully understood the path from freedom to peace and prosperity. He was also disturbed to see the American government travelling down the opposite path.

Due to an international monetary crisis in 1971, President Richard Nixon ordered wage and price controls. He also ended convertibility between US dollars and gold, known as "closing the gold window." For Paul, who was steeped in Austrian economics, these moves amounted to a full frontal assault on economic freedom in America. Worse than that, nobody even seemed aware of the implications.

"I decided to run for Congress because of the disaster of wage and price controls imposed by the Nixon administration in 1971," Paul recalled. "When the stock market responded euphorically to the imposition of these controls and the closing of the gold window, and the US Chamber of Commerce and many other big business groups gave enthusiastic support, I decided that someone in politics had to condemn the controls, and offer the alternative that could explain the past and give hope for the future: the Austrian economists' defense of the free market."

Nixon's economic decisions were bad enough to Paul, but what bothered him even more was that he hardly heard any debate on the matter. Although many people didn't agree with the Nixon administration, what was missing was a principled critique of his government based on the ideal of a free society. Those ideas and values lacked a clear voice in government.

Paul came to a decision. It must have been strange for a small-town doctor with no background in politics and who was, by his very nature, humble and soft-spoken, to sit at his kitchen table and seriously weigh the thought of running for national office. Most congressmen came from wealthy, well-connected families. Paul came from a family of dairy farmers and pastors. Most congressmen have natural constituencies they can tap into. Paul was running precisely because there didn't seem to *be* any constituency for his position.

Nevertheless, he decided that the important part was not to get elected, but to simply air the debate. He knew his election chances were slim, but he could use the opportunity to talk about Austrian economic ideas. Even if he didn't win, his campaign could spread awareness of how a free society works. He ran for office not as a path to Congress, but as a soapbox on which he could air ideas that, so far, weren't getting a hearing.

But Carol didn't quite see it that way, as he would later reveal. "I was looking for a forum to ventilate and politics has allowed me to do that. My goal was not to be in politics or be elected but to present a case for what I thought was important. My wife warned me that it was dangerous because I could end up getting elected. I told her that would never happen!"

He knew his message was unpopular when heard for the first time. Instead of promising handouts and benefits to interest groups, his core proposal was to take the government off everyone's back. He knew this policy would make Americans better off, but it wouldn't sound that way to those hoping to get something for nothing. He believed that the influence of interest groups was much stronger than the force of educated pro-freedom citizens.

Promising to give nothing to people did not seem like a winning strategy. "At the time I was convinced, like Ludwig von Mises, that no one could succeed in politics without serving the special interests of some politically powerful pressure group," he recalled.

Paul launched his political career as a Republican Party candidate for congress. As a Brazoria County resident, he ran to represent Texas's 22nd congressional district, which covers the constituency of the south-central portion of the Houston-Sugar Land-Baytown metropolitan area.

It was a difficult place and time to be a Republican. Not only had the Democrats historically held the district, but the Republicans were having an uncomfortable time with the Watergate scandal and President Nixon's resignation.

None of that stopped Paul from trying. He made his first run for Congress in 1974 against a Democratic incumbent. Paul's campaign slogan was "Freedom, Honesty, and Sound Money", a declaration of the principles upon which he would base his entire career.

Carol's optimism regarding her husband's chances was correct, but her prophecy would not be confirmed right away. Running for the first time on a new message, he faced Robert R. Casey, a senior congressman since 1958. It would be a tough battle to unseat an established incumbent.

After the votes were counted, Casey came out on top, easily retaining his seat with almost 70% of the vote. Paul, who never expected to win, went back to his medical practice and continued studying economics.

In April 1976, over a year after his defeat to Casey, Paul had a second chance at politics, and he had President Gerald Ford to thank for it. Ford was Nixon's Vice President who stepped in after Nixon resigned. He appointed Democrat Casey to the Federal Maritime Commission. Casey accepted, which meant that his seat in congress became vacant. A special election was held specifically to fill the position until the next general election.

Paul saw his chance and put his name on the ballot once again.

His new opponent was a relatively unknown Democrat named Robert Gammage, who had previously served in the local Texas State Senate. Gammage was attempting to go national, moving from state to federal politics.

Democratic opponent Robert Casey

In the previous election, Paul was relatively unknown to voters in the 22nd district compared to the incumbent Casey. However, even though he was soundly defeated by a Democrat in the previous election, he had become a known commodity to voters due to his campaign. It turned out that his campaign not only publicized the message, but the messenger as well. So this time, it was Gammage who was the new face. When the votes were finally counted, Paul was suddenly vaulted into office with 56% of the ballots—a comfortable 12 point spread over his opponent.

The full term for an elected congressman is two years. Paul's first term, however, would be less than a year because his predecessor, Robert Casey, had already served out most of his term. The general election would occur in the same year, leaving him with little more than a semester to make an impact—and that's exactly what he did.

Traveling to Washington was an overwhelming experience for the farm boy who had delivered newspapers to his rural neighbors. Although Paul knew his would be a lonely voice in Washington, his principles were echoed by the monuments dedicated to the founding fathers. Walking around and staring up at the marble statues of his heroes, particularly Thomas Jefferson, he felt not just an opportunity, but a responsibility.

Paul's first day in congress was even more overwhelming. His new workplace at the United States Congress was housed in a single Romanesque building dating back to 1793—the massively domed Capitol Building. The front of the building had 365 steps (one for every day of the year) which Paul made his way up, despite his bad knee. The actual House Chamber, in the south wing of the building, housed all of Paul's fellow Congressmen. In the opposite North wing was the Senate Chamber.

Inside the square House Chamber was a semi-circle of seats for all 435 members of congress. The second level, open to the public, allowed the media and spectators to watch their congressmen in action. Around this second level were 23 stone relief portraits of famous lawmakers throughout history: everyone from Romans in the original Republic to Moses and Napoleon. Of these, two were American: George Mason, the father of the Bill of Rights, and Paul's favorite, Thomas Jefferson, again looking down on him.

Serving in the United States Congress

All 435 seats converged on a large podium, where congressmen stepped forward to deliver their opinions on proposed laws. It was here, in April 1976, that an anxious 40-year-old political novice was sworn into office.

Paul's short first term would be a busy one. He quickly assembled a powerful staff, mostly composed of young intellectuals committed to the cause of freedom. One of the ancillary benefits caused by the dearth of Austrian economics in Congress was that he quickly became its standard-bearer, and he had his pick from the best minds in the field for his staff. Many of them, like Gary North and Bruce Bartlett, had written articles for the *Freeman*, a leading magazine for the freedom cause, read by conservative and libertarian alike.

The young congressman practiced the same decentralized management strategy he advocated for the nation. His style of administration was congruent with his belief in the sheer effectiveness of freedom. Paul hired the best people he could find and left them alone to their work. He knew he could trust them, since he personally selected each one of them.

Gary North, Bruce Bartlett and John Robbins

His office was also highly efficient. Instead of having a bulky staff and an all-controlling Administrative Assistant to make sure everyone was doing his job—a common practice for congressmen—he had a much less bureaucratic organization, in which he kept in personal contact with each of his employees.

Gary North reminisced about their early days together. "When I joined his Congressional staff in June, 1976, he was the most junior member of Congress, having been sworn in only two months earlier. In my tiny three-person office was John W. Robbins, a former student of Hans Sennholz in economics and of Gottfried Dietze in political science. In the main office was Bruce Bartlett, who later became one of the leading defenders in Washington of supply-side economics. This was a high-powered staff for a Congressman with two months' seniority."

As a member of the House of Representatives, Congressman Paul's primary duty was to debate and vote on the approval of all legislative bills. He was also required to take part on a Committee, which is an internal organization that deals with specific tasks. Congressmen may choose which House Committee they want to serve, such as the Agriculture Committee, the Committee on Education and Labor, and so forth.

Paul never forgot that his main reason for entering politics was due to Nixon's decision to close the gold window, so he wouldn't miss a single opportunity of taking his case to Congress. Therefore, he joined the House Committee on Financial Services (also known as the House Banking Committee) which dealt specifically with economic policy and all questions related to financial services.

In June, 1976, Paul had his chance to directly confront the policies he had run for office to decry. Each committee report was accompanied by a minority report, written by those who were in the minority on an issue. Since he was the only congressman to oppose re-financing the International Monetary Fund, he had the opportunity to present a minority report, stating his arguments to the Committee.

North was in charge of writing the report. He later recalled, "The House Banking Committee had been debating the re-financing of the International Monetary Fund (IMF). The ... committee was strongly in favor of putting more taxpayers' money into the relic of the Bretton-Woods monetary conference of 1944. Congressman Paul was the only member of the committee who was opposed to the bill.

"It was my task to write the minority report on Saturday, so that he could hand it in on Monday. ... This minority report so completely amazed the bipartisan establishment that Ron Paul was invited to testify to the *Senate* Banking Committee on his reasons for opposing the funding. I had never heard of this before: a freshman Congressman invited to share his views with a Senate committee. I have not heard of it since."

While Paul was a lonely voice in Congress fighting for tax cuts in the seventies, another school of economic thought was gaining a growing influence advocating a similar position. The supply-side school, which would influence the later Reagan administration, also advocated tax cuts with similar arguments. Like Paul, they argued that less tax would stimulate economic growth, since private individuals would have more money to invest in businesses and careers. In fact, Paul's own employee, Bruce Bartlett, played a major role in the rise of supply-side economics.

However, unlike Paul, supply-siders didn't believe that cutting government spending was equally necessary, because they believed that the economic growth would be enough to pay for the deficit that was being created. Democrats in the media often argued passionately against supply-siders because they believed it would cut down on government revenues. No one ever heard the other argument against supply-side economics by Paul.

His position was clearly different. "Tax relief is important, but members of Congress need to back up tax cuts with spending cuts," he said. "True fiscal conservatism combines both low taxes and low spending."

Paul argued that cutting taxes without cutting spending would lead to a budget deficit that would increase the national debt. While supply-side policies might generate growth in the present, it would only postpone the problem of paying for government expenses. The only difference is that the cost would be deferred, but in every case, Americans would bear the cost.

He argued against supply-side economics from a deep moral perspective—an argument the Tea Party would use decades later. "I disagree with the supply-side argument that government debt doesn't matter," he explained. "Debt does matter, especially to future generations that will be asked to pay for our extravagance. The bills always come due later...responsible people restrain their borrowing because they will have to pay the money back. It's time for American taxpayers to understand that every dollar will have to be repaid. We should have the courage to face our grandchildren knowing that we have done all we can to end the government spending spree."

Besides his activities in Congress, Paul also played an important role in the 1976 presidential election. Before the election, each party conducts a primary election—an internal election through which it selects a nominee. Paul worked as a delegate of the Republican convention; party leaders who are chosen during the primary process and who have the authority to choose the candidate who will represent the party in the general election.

Paul meeting with Ronald Reagan

Paul was not only one of those delegates, but he was the one who led the Texan delegation that supported California Governor Ronald Reagan for president in the National Convention. At the time, he was one of only four congressmen who supported Reagan over Ford. Although Reagan was unsuccessful in the primaries that year (Gerald Ford won), it was an important step for his nomination four years later—and thus it was in many ways the starting point for Reagan's presidency.

Congressman Paul also hadn't forgotten that his decision to enter politics was as much about educating people about liberty as it was about getting elected. In his first months in Congress, he founded the Foundation for Rational Economics Education (FREE), a non-profit, non-partisan, educational foundation dedicated to publishing books and a monthly newsletter. That newsletter, *The Freedom Report*, explained the principles of free-market economics, sound money and limited government.

This unusually busy and active first term, however, would come to an end. Paul had to face Robert Gammage again in the end of 1976. This time, Gammage was more prepared for the election, while Paul was understandably engrossed in his new activities in Washington. What's more, his unconventional positions had raised eyebrows not just in Congress, but back home as well. In a close contest, Paul lost by 268 votes out of 190,000 that were cast. In early 1977, he had to leave DC to go back to his district, his family and his medical practice.

Democratic Opponent R. Gammage

The defeat was a devastating blow to Paul, but in a way, his short political career had been as successful as he could have hoped for when he had contemplated it at his kitchen table with Carol. His campaign had never been about personality. It was about ideas, and his brief time in Congress had done a great deal to advance them. Most importantly, Paul's campaigns and his first term in Washington had laid down the foundation for a network of citizens committed to the cause of freedom, which would prove to be the first step towards larger potential victories down the road.

"My influence, such as it is, comes only by educating others about the rightness of the free market," he said. "The majority of the voters in my district have approved, as have those familiar with free-market economics. And voters in other districts, encouraged by my speaking out for freedom and sound money, influence their representatives in the direction of a free market. My influence comes through education, not the usual techniques of a politician. But the more usual politicians in Congress will hardly solve our problems. Americans need a better understanding of Austrian economics."

And, while the decision he had made in 1971 had been a difficult, even eccentric one, as he returned to his practice in Texas, he privately vowed that someday he'd return to Washington. He had come to believe that, in the long run, the campaigns could prove to be more than a political contest for a seat in Congress; they could be the beginning of a much larger movement. Decades later, Paul himself would remark, "The flowering of human society depends on two factors: the intellectual power of outstanding men to conceive sound social and economic theories, and the ability of these or other men to make these ideologies palatable to the majority." This would become his life's work, and in that regard, he was already a success.

Paul's defeat was offset by a happy announcement in 1977. Oldest daughter Lori Paul became engaged to Tom Pyeatt. Ron and Carol could soon look forward to an even larger family.

Chapter 8

Ron Paul's heartrending photo-finish defeat in the election of 1976 returned him to his medical practice in Lake Jackson, Texas. In reality he had never really left; he had only taken three months off from his practice to campaign for the special election earlier in 1976.

By January 1977, he was back full-time, and still not taking any federal dollars. The rejection of government money did not impair his financial success. According to partner Jack Pruett, "we had a pretty busy practice, and a pretty lucrative practice."

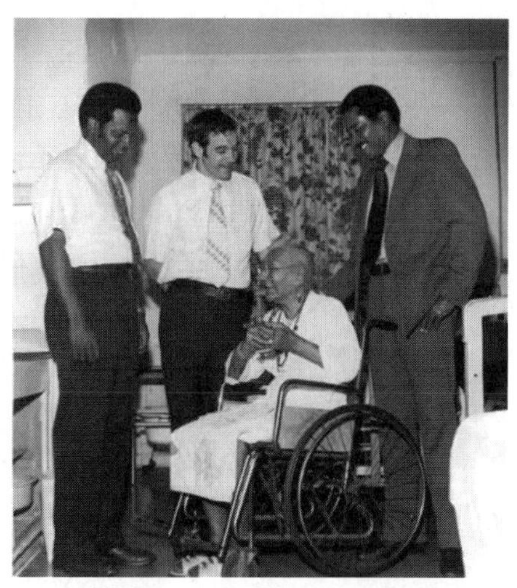

Paul returning to medicine

Due to the closeness of the previous electoral contest, Paul knew he would attempt to unseat Robert Gammage in the next election. The incumbent Democrat probably felt confident because Republican morale was still low following Nixon's resignation. There was no reason to doubt that the tradition of Democratic representatives in the district would continue.

In 1978, Paul was back on the campaign trail, working even harder than before. "He was a great politician," recalls Paul's future chief of staff, Lew Rockwell. "He'd wear out three or four pairs of shoes walking neighborhoods." People were inclined to listen because "he has heavy content in everything he says. He's a great teacher."

It didn't hurt that his medical practice had already won over most of the young families in the district. "I had real difficulty down in Brazoria County where he practiced," Gammage told National Public Radio, referring to his contests against Paul. "Because he delivered half the babies in the county. There were only two OB/GYNs in the county and the other one was his partner."

It was their third contest in as many election cycles. The calm and polite doctor ran a tough and aggressive campaign, surprising his opponent. The campaign team knew it would be a close election. Two years earlier, he narrowly lost reelection to Gammage by 268 votes in the recount vote. This time, Paul's extra campaigning paid off. He overtook Gammage and won the 1978 rematch by a slightly wider margin—a mere 1,200 votes.

Now Paul had more time to assemble his congressional staff than his previous term. Bruce Bartlett, the supply-sider who worked for him in 1976, did not return. Instead, Bartlett went to work for Jack Kemp, a fellow Republican congressman.

For his chief of staff, Paul asked for a recommendation from Leonard Read, the founder of FEE. Read recommended 34-year-old Llewellyn Rockwell, a fellow student of Austrian Economics. Intensely rational, Rockwell had the ability to counter critics of the free market with a passionate response backed up by a diverse set of historical examples. This ability won him the additional role of speechwriter.

"I loved working for Ron," says Rockwell. "What you see is what you get. He really is the same in private as he is in public."

Although he shared a similar belief system with Paul, the two men had contrasting personalities. Paul exhibited a gentlemanly grace when disagreeing with his opponents, whereas Rockwell could be harsh and dismissive. In Paul's world there were no bad people, just sincere but misguided individuals. In Rockwell's world, there were villains. He called those who benefit from the Federal Reserve "monsters" and labeled his opponents "fascists". The fire that kept his fight going had a different temperature from that of Paul. His rhetoric clearly showed the outrage he felt towards the people who were, as he saw it, ruining a once great nation.

Rockwell saw his time in Washington as an educational mission. "We never saw his office as a conventionally political one," he explains. "It was a bully pulpit to get the message out. We sent out hundreds of thousands of tracts on freedom, inserted amazing articles in the Congressional Record, and drafted libertarian legislation as an educational effort."

Congressman Paul's first full term focused primarily on three issues: his passionate opposition to the Monetary Control Act of 1980, a restoration of the gold standard, and opposition to restoration of the military draft.

The life of a congressman is demanding, yet Paul continued to work part-time at his medical practice. "He was quite amazing in how much energy he had," Dr. Pruett recalls. "Out in Washington, they didn't believe in working on Fridays. Every Friday morning he'd hop on a plane and come home and see patients by Friday afternoon." If necessary, he worked all day Saturday as well. "Bright and early Monday morning, he'd get back on a plane to Washington."

For Dr. Paul, medicine was his primary vocation. "That was Ron's profession and I honestly believe that was what he wanted. He didn't want to be a politician," says Pruitt.

Paul lost no time after his election in aligning himself with like-minded men and women on both sides of the aisle in Congress. It was no surprise that one of these allies was a fellow physician, the conservative Georgia Democrat Dr. Larry McDonald. The two physicians were outwardly much alike. Both were young for politicians, serving in Congress after successful medical careers (McDonald was an urologist). They were also devotees of the Austrian School of economics, whose policies included the preservation of national sovereignty.

McDonald was a high-ranking member of the militantly anti-communist John Birch Society, and eventually became the organization's president. Paul frequented John Birch Society dinners as a speaker, and some of his congressional staff had been drawn from the ranks of professionals who had served at the Society's headquarters in Belmont, Massachusetts. This included Lew Rockwell, who had briefly worked in Belmont, as well as Legislative Assistant John W. Robbins.

Paul's Democratic ally Larry McDonald

"They were very good friends," recalled Rockwell of the two doctors. "They both had the same view of medicine and how government was an intrusion in it." Paul and McDonald, along with two other Texas congressmen (Democrat Marvin Leath and Republican John M. Collins) voted against compensating Iranian embassy hostages on December 18, 1979. The two doctors stood virtually alone in the lopsided 369-4 vote, arguing that the mere fact that the hostages had gone through hardship did not earn them the right to pick the taxpayers' pocketbooks. Paul told the Philadelphia Inquirer that McDonald had been the most conservative congressman in the House and "he was the most principled, too."

But Paul and McDonald had their differences as well, Rockwell stresses. "They were allied on domestic affairs, but, of course, not allies on military policy."

McDonald was strongly anti-communist. Ironically, a journey later in his career to speak out against communism would result in a dramatic and untimely end to his congressional career.

But before that event would occur, the conservative Southern Democrat recoiled at the restrictions put upon the intelligence establishment in the wake of the Senate's intelligence review (known as the Church Committee) in the mid-1970s. Paul took a skeptical view toward intelligence bureaucracies and instead put a premium on personal privacy. And McDonald supported a restoration of the military draft along the lines of the Swiss model, arguing that "The all-volunteer military force is an alternative to a draft, but it is an expensive way to go. … [T]here are serious questions as to whether a paycheck is an adequate substitute for patriotic fervor."

In January 1979, at the time Paul returned to Congress, the military draft was no distant memory. It had been repealed less than six years earlier at the close of the Vietnam conflict, having been a political fixture for decades before that. Democratic leaders began campaigning to bring back the draft in order to avoid being painted as soft on communism.

Paul quickly took up the issue as many of his colleagues sought to force a return of conscription. Many—like McDonald—employed Cold War arguments that the quality or costs of the military in an all-volunteer force would endanger national security, or that youth owe their country mandatory service. Paul countered, "If a nation is free and morally and spiritually strong, the people will provide an adequate military for national defense. A draft will not substitute for, nor create, a morally and spiritually strong nation. Force cannot overcome apathy." He pointed out that a draft is only necessary for an aggressive military, adding that early in US history when the nation had been invaded, the Republic had more than enough volunteers to repel the invaders. Only in non-defensive wars was a draft necessary.

But Paul reserved his strongest criticisms for the argument that youth owed their government service, as conservatives sometimes argued. He pointed out that conservatives who made this argument morally disarmed themselves for liberal assaults on their wallet, saying, "The assumption is that the young, age 17 to 24, owe a segment of their lives to their country. This assumption is based upon the supposition that rights come from the state and are not natural. It also assumes that life itself is a privilege and not something that we are absolutely entitled to. … Once this is granted, the conservatives have no defense against the liberal notion that the more productive have an obligation and therefore must be compelled to care for those who won't work or can't work."

As always, at the bottom of Paul's argument was the Constitution. "Our Constitution prohibits involuntary servitude and the Declaration of Independence has declared to all mankind that we are endowed by our Creator with the inalienable rights of life and liberty. With this heritage, the draft and compulsory national service are unacceptable." Paul declared the draft "a form of slavery" and "a waste of money" in a front page *Washington Post* story.

According to Rockwell, he worked closely with Pat Schroeder (D-Colorado) and David Stockman (R-Michigan) to fight a restoration of the draft. "They were the three key people." The alliance worked, despite the fact that Pat Schroeder was one of the most liberal members of the House and Stockman an old-style moderate Republican (though he had styled himself part of the New Right). Facing highly public, vocal opposition from this ideological mishmash of liberal Democrats, moderate Republicans and the "right-winger" Paul, the Democrat-controlled Congress dropped the measure.

Despite differences with McDonald on the draft and the intelligence establishment, the two doctors often co-sponsored each other's bills, thereby gaining instant bipartisanship for their respective legislation. Paul regularly co-sponsored McDonald's legislation to get the US out of the United Nations.

Both men had always been dogged opponents of international governmental banking institutions. Foremost among these institutions was the International Monetary Fund (IMF), established in 1944. The other was the World Bank, organized in 1945. Both institutions were UN backed creatures of the Bretton-Woods agreement.

His arguments against globalist institutions included his sincere belief that they were contributing to economic misery. But his most essential objection rested on the Constitution. "Our Constitution does not give us the authority to sell our sovereignty to an international government body, and even under the treaty provisions of the Constitution it is not permissible. The treaty provision does not allow us, for example, to undermine the Bill of Rights."

Paul showed no fear of congressional leaders or powerful establishment figures during his first full term in Congress. Other politicians routinely traveled to congressional junkets abroad, which they called "fact-finding missions." Asked by the *Washington Post* what he thought of these junkets, Paul didn't hesitate to call it a waste of money. "That's what we have ambassadors for," he told the Post.

Paul had also garnered a reputation for going after targets that were barely on other people's political radars. A prime example in 1980 was the Export-Import Bank of the United States. Known as the Ex-Im bank, it was established in 1934 by an executive order from Franklin Roosevelt as part of his New Deal plan. The purpose of the Ex-Im bank was to finance and insure foreign purchases of US goods for customers unable or unwilling to accept credit risk, all in the name of increasing US exports.

Decades after it had been established, Paul noticed the Ex-Im bank was actually helping the United States' cold war opponent. Years later, he wrote to then President Reagan, telling him, "Through the Ex-Im Bank, we are right now financing Yugoslavia's purchase and development of advanced telecommunications systems, computers, sophisticated aircraft, even nuclear power plants—all of which could conceivably be used for military purposes. This policy is suicidal and must be stopped."

Paul accepted the argument of the Austrian economists that a regulated, centrally controlled economy was not sustainable. Without US taxpayer support, he argued, the Soviet bloc would collapse economically—an argument that was later proved in the early 1990's.

Paul's consistent votes on principle and his refusal to be carried away with partisan bickering led to a strange paradox. He was personally popular with the other congressmen, especially during congressional softball games where he was one of the stars. But while he was well liked by almost everybody, he had very few political allies in Washington. "He was friendly with everyone," Rockwell explains. "But he was ideologically a loner."

He was an ideological loner because he criticized the actions of those in his own Republican Party as stiffly as those of the Democrats. He criticized President Nixon's wage and price controls as fervently as President Carter's profligate spending policies.

Nevertheless, those few members of Congress who did ally with him found his diligence and earnestness refreshing. His key ally and friend in the House remained Larry McDonald. They had agreed with one another enough to help each other in congress, yet their disagreements provided for lively conversations. Unfortunately, years later, their friendship was cut tragically short.

Both McDonald and Senator Jesse Helms were invited to South Korea for the 30th anniversary of the Mutual Defense Treaty. McDonald missed one of his connecting flights due to poor weather and instead booked a flight aboard Korean Airlines Flight 007. During the flight, the Korean pilot went off course into Soviet Airspace and was subsequently shot down by a Soviet MIG, killing all 240 passengers and 29 crew, including McDonald.

Although many criticized the over-reaction by the Soviets, Paul pointed out the broader picture of the tragedy, observing that the United States Ex-Im Bank had provided funds that could have conceivably been used to build the MIG that shot down the airliner. He wrote to President Reagan, "The Soviet bloc already owes the West $100 billion; that has purchased many MIG-23s and SU-15s."

McDonald was well known for introducing bills that opposed the United Nations. After his death, Paul carried on his fight. He even introduced his own bill, The American Sovereignty Restoration Act (HR 1146) to withdraw the US from the United Nations. Even in his later years in congress, Paul bi-annually introduced HR 1146, which would terminate the nation's UN membership and invalidate all UN diplomats' immunity.

Much later, he introduced HR 3090 in January of 1998, which would have ended US membership in the IMF. He also sponsored bills to withdraw from UNESCO (an agency of the UN) and to invalidate the International Criminal Court. Through these actions, he carried on McDonald's legacy by fighting for issues important to his Democratic colleague.

Chapter 9

The early 1980s were a golden age for Ron Paul; not in the conventional sense but instead as a description of his devoted campaign to resurrect gold as a monetary form of exchange. The first step towards this goal began with a close race for his congressional seat.

Paul's opponent for reelection was Democrat Mike Andrews, a former assistant district attorney for Harris County. Beyond his public sector credentials, Andrews had experience working for a private law firm in the Houston area. His campaign came armed with an established reputation and a war chest dwarfing Paul's funds.

Congressman Paul's previous election had been tight and certain incumbency was far from established at this point. Many analysts still viewed him as a flash in the pan; a short respite from the Democratic Party's long held dominance of the 22nd district. This election would decide whether the Democrats could once again reign supreme in the region. The alternative was to acknowledge a deep-rooted shift in the district's politics.

Democratic Opponent Mike Andrews

Andrews' funding was easily $100,000 more than Paul's. His familiarity with the Houston area threatened Paul, who generally garnered the majority of his support from the southern parts of the district. Despite these electoral obstacles, Paul gave a strong challenge.

In third place was Vaudie Nance, an independent registering only a thousand votes. Paul held 51.04% of the vote while his challenger clutched an impressive 48.31%. Separating Paul and defeat were only 5,704 votes. He had maintained his Congressional seat by yet another slim margin.

His opponent too would eventually continue a fruitful political career in a neighboring district. Andrews went on to win the 1982 House of Representatives seat for the 25th Texas district in the nearby Austin area. Here, Andrews would represent the district for a dozen years until 1995, finally ending his role in politics after a failed Senate seat attempt.

In 1981, sweetening Paul's victory was the birth of Matthew, his first grandchild from his oldest daughter Lori and husband, Tom Pyeatt. Little did Paul know that Matt would be the first of seventeen grandchildren.

Paul hitting a home run

In Washington, Paul was a star player at the annual Congressional Baseball Game. Playing for the Republican team at Four Mile Run Park, he had the distinction of being the only congressman to ever hit a home run over the fence. "He could have been a professional baseball player if he had not had a knee injury," Lew Rockwell says.

For Paul, it seemed like a good year to be a Republican as Ronald Reagan's election shook the political arena to its core. Reagan and Paul were political allies who helped each other early in their respective careers. Placing such an important ally in the White House opened a window of opportunity for bold new actions. Reagan would soon demonstrate that he had the political will to dramatically alter the course of America. His strength was exhibited early in his presidency when the PATCO union (Professional Air

Traffic Controllers Organization) organized a nation-wide strike.

PATCO had uncharacteristically backed Reagan, the Republican candidate, for the 1980 election. Despite its support, the president used federal authority to break the strike and fire 11,000 workers unwilling to return to their government-monopoly jobs, which were unfortunately necessary for the national economy. Few men in history have had the political clout to turn against their own constituents, especially powerful unions. Reagan had demonstrated a strong determination to change how things were done in Washington.

Meeting with President Reagan aboard Air Force One

With Reagan in office it seemed like change was possible, and returning to gold currency seemed within reach. Since Nixon's 1971 decision, the US dollar had been completely floated on the confidence in the United States government and economy. The last ties with gold and the dollar were severed. After abandoning all traces of gold, the US experienced a decade of stagflation—increasing inflation accompanied by rising unemployment. Unprecedented financial performance of precious commodities on the stock market reinforced the gold movement. On January 21, 1980, gold hit a peak of $850 and would not reach the same nominal state until January 3rd, 2008. With these unusual and disconcerting market conditions, the climate was ripe for drastic change.

Paul was one of the only politicians who understood the damage caused by inflationary policy. In a timely quote, he explained, "Interventionist economists carelessly criticize the spreading of economic growth through a free-market society as the 'trickle-down theory.' But inflation, by trickling, then rushing through society, spreads economic misery among the poor, working, and middle classes, while enriching the special interests. It is this 'trickling-down' that deserves condemnation from everyone concerned about poverty."

Even the US Treasury held reservations about a free floating dollar unfettered by gold. Treasury Under-Secretary Anthony Solomon admitted to Congress, "Gold remains a significant part of the reserves of central banks available in times of need. This is unlikely to change in the foreseeable future." Paul viewed this position as inherently contradictory; if paper money was truly an elite monetary medium, there should have been no need for the central banks to store gold reserves in "times of need."

Paul, through the help of his non-profit organization, FREE (Foundation for Rational Economics and Education), began organizing dinners in order to foster an educated and informed political body on the topic of gold. The dinners invited presidential aides and administrative officials in an effort to increase support for the gold movement. Aiding this goal was Paul's *Freedom Report* published and distributed by FREE.

With the intention of assisting gold legislation, FREE published Paul's book, *Gold, Peace, and Prosperity*. This short text summarized the history and problems associated with fiat money and offered as a solution a 100% gold-backed dollar. Among the oft quoted economists in the book was Dr. Murray Rothbard, who wrote the introduction. Economic commentator and journalist, Henry Hazlitt, added the preface.

The elevated price of gold, threatening inflation, and the building momentum of FREE's efforts facilitated the beginnings of serious debate in Congress regarding the future of the precious metal. The movement had recent legislative successes. In October 1977, Senator Jesse Helms of North Carolina managed to pass a bill permitting gold clauses in private contracts. And, during that period, he also began pushing for the creation of a gold commission. Helms was an invaluable ally for Paul as both men were strong believers in the free market. In fact, the Council for a Competitive Economy identified Paul as having the highest percentage of votes for free economic competition in the House of Representatives at 91%. Helms similarly ranked at the top among Senators.

With the election of Ronald Reagan, "gold bugs" like Rep. Paul and Senator Helms finally found a platform.

On October 7, 1980, at President Reagan's behest, Congress formed the Gold Commission in order to explore and study the role of gold in domestic and international monetary systems. Unfortunately, one problem with the Gold Commission—as with any commission—was that it was possible to stack the members in favor of one policy over another, thereby guaranteeing the outcome before testimony even began.

As the principal gold standard advocate in Congress, Paul was appointed as a member. Unfortunately for him, he was the only congressional member publicly on the record as favoring the gold standard. In addition to members of the house, the last four seats of the sixteen-person committee went to academics and private businessmen. Among the businessmen were gold dealer Herbert Coyne and former Rite-Aid corporation president Lewis Lehrman. The academics consisted of Arthur Costamangna, an economist and former chair of the Council of Economic Advisors, and Anna Schwartz, an extremely knowledgeable economist best known for co-authoring *A Monetary History of the United States* with Nobel Prize winner Milton Friedman.

To many outside observers, the selection process appeared suspect. A pair of writers for *The Washington Post* wrote about the commission's biases in their article "Enemies of Gold." Quoting a high ranking administration official, the writers noticed "that this commission won't cause any trouble." The journalists clarified the situation by observing, "No chances were taken. Out of the 16 commission members, only two favor a gold standard—Rep. Paul and Lewis Lehrman."

The first glimmers of hope for a discussion favorable to the possibility of returning to the gold standard fell apart early on. As *The Washington Post* noted, "The attention the Gold Commission is attracting, in the view of economist Alan Greenspan, 'has a lot to do with things other than gold.' Greenspan thinks that the commission will stimulate 'a dialogue showing general dissatisfaction on the way the whole financial system is working.'" But not necessarily a dialogue regarding the gold standard.

The chosen congressmen were hardly amicable to Paul's views, and the Democratic members—Stephen Neal (North Carolina), Chris Dodd (Connecticut), and Henry Reuss (Wisconsin)—were particularly antagonistic towards a gold standard. Although Dodd was one of the most far-left voting members in Congress, the real threat was Henry Reuss.

Congressman Paul called Reuss "the most anti-gold person in Washington." Demonstrating his distaste for the commodity, Reuss behaved childishly during Gold Commission meetings. The Wall Street Journal reported his behavior by printing, "The meeting began with Rep. Henry Reuss, a vocal opponent of the gold standard, crumpling a copy of *Hard Money News*, a pro-gold newsletter, and throwing it on the floor. The Wisconsin Democrat said he objected to the newsletter characterizing Federal Reserve Chairman Paul Volcker as 'a proven liar every time he opens his mouth.'"

The decision to include three Federal Reserve governors was particularly troubling to Paul because it was effectively like allowing bank robbers to juror their own trial. Their preset animosity was displayed throughout the process, especially by Emmett Rice and Henry Wallich.

Emmett Rice revealed to the commission that he "believes issue of rules vs. discretion is subject for another commission. The commission should not make recommendations on monetary rule or how to run the current system."

Anna Schwartz, recognizing Wallich's prejudices, noted, "Their primary concern was to limit discussion touching on the performance of the Federal Reserve. Governor Wallich argued at the first meeting that the subjects of inflation and monetary policy were not a proper concern of the Commission."

According to the Federal Reserve governors, the Gold Commission created to study the role of gold in domestic and international monetary systems could not discuss inflation, Federal Reserve rules, or monetary policy. Although there were no official guidelines of narrow macroeconomic topics, the Federal Reserve participants desired to avoid all critical debate of the Fed's performance.

Dr. Schwartz herself was not supportive of Paul's cause either. In her *Reflections on the Gold Commission Report*, Schwartz summarized his views as purely a belief in the Constitution, brushing aside his other objections. She wrote, "They are obviously constructed from libertarian principles and a belief in the superiority of commodity money." Contradicting her statement in the same article, she admitted Paul's "case for the gold standard is based on historical, theoretical, economic, and moral grounds." Further, she complimented his work by praising a "generally high level of scholarship, on US money and banking history in the nineteenth and twentieth centuries." This was true praise from the economist who wrote *A Monetary History of the United States*, a near Biblical tome for professional economists.

The few gold standard supporters on the committee weren't particularly helpful to Paul's cause. Lewis Lehrman and Arthur Costamagna believed in a gold standard melding the dollar to a fixed exchange ratio with gold, despite the fact that a similar fixed exchange rate managed by the Federal Reserve led to the deepening of the Great Depression.

Paul's ultimate goal was the Gold Standard alone, without the Federal Reserve fixed exchange ratio. He believed the paper money supported by the Federal Reserve was a bad option, but the Federal Reserve existing parallel to the Gold Standard was about the worst combination possible. This focus on an obviously flawed version of the Gold Standard allowed the opposition to concentrate on others' erroneous views instead of acknowledging Paul's separate version of gold money.

Although Paul, Lehrman, and Costamagna did not agree on their respective visions of the gold standard, they formed an alliance of sorts. This alliance was largely based on their agreement to a secondary aspect of the Gold Commission: introducing an American investment grade coin to compete with the popular South African Krugerrand. The creation of an American gold coin was generally favored by the entire Commission, but most feverishly promoted by the gold alliance.

During the commission, some members claimed not to understand the difference between Lehrman's gold standard views and Paul's, which was surprising considering the high level of economic literacy on the panel. Noticing the disagreements, President Reagan told reporters that, "they can't even agree on historical facts."

Unfortunately, Reagan's support for gold was lukewarm. While campaigning earlier, he had supported a gold standard. Since the presidential election, his rhetoric on gold died down to practical silence. While supporting the gold standard in private, he refused to speak out in public.

As the Gold Commission floundered, Paul turned to the president to make a strong public statement in support of the gold position. Unfortunately, Reagan was beginning to see Paul as less of an ally than in previous years. The two shared a common belief in free market principles, but Reagan also believed in the need for a strong military buildup against the USSR. He frequently called upon Paul to support new Department of Defense projects.

"Some people hate Ron Paul because he can't be bought," begins Rockwell. "I remember working for him in Washington one night late in the office when Reagan called him. This time he was putting unbelievable pressure on Ron to vote for some horrible new bomber. Ron wouldn't do it. They all eventually learned that his arm is un-twistable."

Paul's tendency to say no made it hard for other political allies to say yes to him. During a 10-minute helicopter ride from the White House, he intercepted the president, seeking a public show of support for the gold standard. Understandably, Reagan was not very accommodating. However, he told Paul that he still supported the Gold Standard and still hoped for a favorable outcome.

Anna Schwartz speculated that if Reagan openly and boldly made a stance on gold, the votes in the commission could have gone quite differently. All four Republicans would submit to his backing as well as his economic advisors. Further, three of the four private citizens could have been convinced by such authority. Without the president's approval, no one wanted to align themselves with the underdog, Ron Paul.

After nine meetings, with 23 witnesses testifying before the panel, the Gold Commission finally voted 15 to 2 against the recommendation to allow dollars to be convertible into gold. Favorably, 12 to 3 voted to recommend the minting of a new gold coin from the Treasury surplus. One of the three opposed to this move was Henry Reuss, detesting every possible aspect of gold.

On March 31, 1982, the Gold Commission issued two reports: the majority report and the minority report of Costamagna, Lehrman, and Paul. The minority report was surprisingly large, considering only three members endorsed the text. Endorsement does not necessarily mean direct support, however—the greater part was penned by Paul and represents his view on gold, not Lehrman's nor Costamagna's. Their acknowledgement was more a representation of solidarity in the greater struggle to promote gold than a true meeting of minds.

With the Gold Commission closed, Paul looked to reelection for his third term in 1982. His previous opponent, Mike Andrews, had left for the 25th district, leaving the 22nd uncontested. Paul's district was the only Texas congressional seat without opposition, including independent, libertarian, or socialist candidates. The official election records show 943 opposing write-in votes and 66,536 votes supporting Paul. It was clear he had finally solidified his position in congress. He had, in his anti-establishment way, nevertheless managed to become part of the establishment.

Paul's Chief of Staff, Lew Rockwell, was himself becoming disillusioned by working within the establishment. "I eventually got to the point where it was slightly difficult for me to work for the government, even though it was Ron," he says. "I kept telling myself the House is not as bad as the Presidency." Rockwell departed Paul's staff at the end of 1982 and soon thereafter founded the Ludwig von Mises Institute to promote Austrian economics.

Despite ultimately being a bust as far as gold bugs were concerned, the Gold Commission did manage to create some beneficial results. Media attention to gold monetary issues prior to the commission was nonexistent, but the meetings reawakened serious academic debate. This wasn't merely a discussion amongst Austrian economists; it challenged the politically diverse mainstream views of Robert Hall, Anna Schwartz, Robert Mundell, and Arthur Laffer.

The commission's recommendation for a gold coin resulted in bills HR 1662 and 1663, along with Senate S 42, producing

American Gold Eagles, one of the world's most respected investment grade coins. Afterwards, the Cato Institute published *The Case for Gold* in 1982, with the assistance of John Robbins, Christopher Weber, and Murray Rothbard. The book consists of Paul's minority report to the Gold Commission, with extra additions contributed by his three associates. In 1983, Paul would publish *Ten Myths About Paper Money*, dealing with common misconceptions on the issue. The book demonstrated his determination to keep fighting, publishing, and staying hopeful for the future despite his recent failures with the Gold Commission.

Chapter 10

While Ron Paul had become the gold standard's most effective advocate post-Nixon, he remained frustrated by how easily he was marginalized or ignored in the House of Representatives. He was thinking of ways to advance his agenda when an opportunity presented itself in 1984.

That year, Senator John Tower announced his decision to retire after 22 years due to being "fed up" with a "multi-layered bureaucracy" in Washington. Tower had been the first Republican Senator from Texas in the 20th century—he held Lyndon Johnson's old seat—and with his unexpected departure, the race quickly shaped up to be one of the most competitive in the country. There seemed a strong chance that the Democrats might regain their dynasty controlling both Texas Senate seats. Tower's previous race was a close call, winning with only 12,000 votes—a 0.3 percent lead. The razor-thin victory gave both Democrats and Republicans an equal opportunity to capture the seat.

As opposed to being one voice in a choir of 435 congressmen, the Senate would afford Paul a larger soapbox and the potential to dictate the debate. In a narrowly divided Senate—which was split 55-45 in favor of the GOP at the time—his voice would be difficult to ignore. If a vote on a bill resulted in a near tie, Paul's vote, and voice, would be more powerful still, acting as a tie breaker in the process, and giving him almost the same power as a presidential veto. Few politicians were bold enough to vote against their party. Even fewer did so when their vote could change the course of legislation. However, Paul had no reservations in doing so in order to stick to his principled dedication to the Constitution.

With the chance to make a significant difference in politics and to raise the profile of the issues he cared about, Paul decided to go for it. He jumped into the race ahead of his opponents and announced his candidacy. Others soon followed.

The Republican contenders who joined Paul in the primary race were Robert Mosbacher Jr., a Texas oil man with little political experience; Henry Grover, an uninspiring politician with absolute allegiance to Ronald Reagan; and Phil Gramm, a fellow Texas congressman and economist.

Republican primary opponent Phil Gramm

Gramm had recently caused a stir. He had begun his career in the House as a Democrat, and served on the Democratic Budget Committee. But during the 1980s he had drifted far to the right, heavily favoring Reagan's economic policies and siding with the administration over his party more often than not. Gramm's roguishness even extended to the point of divulging secrets from the Democrat Budget Committee to the GOP. Using a rarely executed option, the Democrats removed Gramm from his position on the committee. Encountering open hostility from his party, he infamously switched sides. As a new Republican, he was re-elected to the House of Representatives with a special election and was now eyeing bigger prizes in the Senate.

Gramm's political stance could be seen as a harbinger of things to come in the Republican Party. As the neoconservative movement later grew, the lines between liberals and conservatives in the two-party sense became blurred (Gramm would later become one of John McCain's economic advisors during the 2008 presidential campaign). The list of characters in the neo-Conservative movement is a list of who's who on Gramm's 1984 campaign bandwagon.

Among them were Karl Rove and Paul Weywich, CEO of the Free Congress Research Education Foundation.

On the Democratic side were far left-wing Lloyd Doggett, former congressman Bob Krueger (who was said to have never stopped campaigning since his defeat in the previous election) and Kent Hance, a Texan breed of very conservative Democrats often referred to as "boll weevils" in that state's politics.

The Democratic race was evenly matched among the three. For this reason, it was difficult for Republican candidates to focus on any one opponent from the Democratic side. This led the Republican primaries to largely focus on their own candidates instead of comparing conservative candidates to liberal counterparts.

Paul's views differed vastly from his opponents'. He was against practically all government intervention, especially with regard to foreign policy. Referring to South American interventionism, he openly made his stance during a debate with the other contenders by stating, "We don't interfere, we don't meddle, we don't send the C.I.A. out to murder people." During the race, the US still had troops in Lebanon and was actively retaliating against Hezbollah for the 1983 Beirut bombing of the international forces barracks leading to the deaths of 241 American servicemen. Interventionism was, in fact, something the Republican Party was actively defending at the time.

It was a primary climate distinctly unfavorable to Paul's brand of non-interventionism, but he nevertheless persisted, as his campaign chose to attack Gramm (and by extension, other supporters of Reagan-era interventions) on foreign policy. He ran a television ad proclaiming, "Vote for Gramm and keeping the marines in Lebanon indefinitely or vote for Paul and bringing them home." His opponent criticized Paul for not standing with Reagan on this issue, and GOP partisans constantly accused him of disloyalty. With a bit of circumstantial irony, only eight days later on February 7, 1984, Reagan announced that the US would begin to withdraw troops from Lebanon.

During the 1980s, Paul had a different reputation compared to his later political career, when his credibility as a Republican fell into question. While he was often attacked for his disinterest in partisanship (that is, voting for the good of the Republican Party), nobody denied his conservative credentials. In fact, he was just as likely to be attacked for being *too* conservative. In the 1984 election, Paul was said to be "ultra-conservative", "...a Republican whose conservatism is so extreme...", and "a far-right wing politician who breathes fire against government regulation of anything." The National Taxpayers Union acknowledged him as the "most ardent anti-spender in Congress." This was in contrast to Gramm, whose conservative credentials were constantly under fire, leaving him to defend himself against charges that he was what would later be called a RINO—Republican In Name Only.

One factor added even more pressure to the campaigns of both Gramm and Paul. At the time, Texas electoral laws held that no candidate could be in two races on the same Texas ballot. In order to run for Senate, both candidates had to give up their seats in the House of Representatives and not stand for reelection. This made the election between the two main candidates an all-or-nothing contest. Whoever fell short of victory in the Senate primary would be out of office for at least two years.

Paul didn't hold back his views in the election. He expressed them unapologetically at debates, while Gramm even avoided attending the debates. For example, Reagan at the time was in full support of the Nicaraguan Contras, as well as giving military aid to countries in the region such as El Salvador. He also funded South American countries to combat drugs. It was politically dangerous to oppose these views for a Republican in 1984, but that's exactly what Paul did.

The rift between Paul and the Reagan administration deepened when First Lady Nancy Reagan took on illicit drug abuse with an awareness campaign under the slogan "Just Say No." The slogan caught on and spread like wildfire, making her program one of the most publicized awareness campaigns ever. Paul agreed with her philosophy, as he too recognized illicit drug use by young people as potentially harmful, but he disagreed about the means to achieving those ends.

Just Say No would have been fine with the majority of libertarians. After all, voluntary choice is the unifying idea of the freedom philosophy. The Reagan administration, however, thought differently. They used the heavy hand of government and the full force of criminal law to coerce the public to say no, resulting in tens of thousands of arguably victimless offenders being jailed.

By 1984, the drug war was in full swing, both at home and abroad. Yet Congressman Paul remained steadfast in his ideals. Unfortunately, his campaign was in an era without discussion and debate on the subject. Illicit drugs—particularly the cheap, potent form of cocaine popular in inner cities known as crack—were viewed as an absolute evil that must be eradicated at all costs. And there were almost no voices in electoral politics willing to risk being labeled as "pro-drugs."

In the Democratic race, the election results brought the three candidates remarkably close to one another. Each candidate had 31% of the vote with the differences measured in decimals. A runoff was held proclaiming Lloyd Doggett the winner.

The votes on the Republican side did not count favorably for Paul. In last place was Henry Grover at 2.5% followed closely by Robert Mosbacher with 7.8%. Paul managed to accumulate 55,431 votes giving him 16.5%. Gramm, on the other hand, swept the primary with a definitive 73.3%. He went on to defeat Lloyd Doggett in the main election with 59%. The Democrat turned Republican won the seat which, itself, had been Democrat turned Republican.

As for Paul's vacated seat in the House, the absence of an incumbent cleared the way for a number of relatively unknown local candidates to throw their hats in the ring, resulting in a crowded, six-way Republican primary. The winner of that primary, who went on to win the seat, was a young member of the Texas House of Representatives named Tom DeLay.

Paul's calculated risk had failed, and he once again found himself a political outsider. His farewell address to Congress cast him as a man frustrated with what he had been unable to accomplish in his time there, and most of all, disillusioned by the difficulty he encountered broaching certain topics. In his view, there was no allowable questioning of foreign policy on either side of the isle, "no dissent is permissible and all true debate is squelched."

Paul vented his feelings to the congressmen present at his address. "Instead of asking which form of intervention and planning government should impose, perhaps someday Congress will debate intervention versus nonintervention, government versus voluntary planning, US sovereignty versus internationalism—the pros and cons of true liberty. Today the debate basically is only that of deciding who will be the victims and who the beneficiaries. "

Paul's farewell was also cynical about the contradictory nature of conservatives and liberals. One conservative would lambaste the subsidies of another as anti-market while protecting his own special interest subsidies. Logical consistency was absent in Washington decision-making. He pointed out, "Good conservatives explain why guns and teachers shouldn't be registered, and beg and plead and coerce the government into registering their own kids for the draft."

He also noted the inconsistency of foreign policy. "South Africa, for their defective system of civil liberties, is banned from the Olympics, while we beg the murdering Communists to come."

He specifically targeted liberals, who he believed "show greater concern for the lives of seals than for the life of a human baby." The farewell address left no stone unturned and no hypocrisy unrevealed. It was perhaps uncharacteristically bitter, but more heart-felt than his regular speeches to congress.

To Paul, the virtues of liberty seemed all but lost in Congress, with their lack of concern for indebting future generations. He remarked, "Those not willing to vote for the cuts either must believe they are not a threat or do not care if they are. I suspect the former to be the case." He noted that on Capitol Hill, "the defender of liberty is seen as bizarre."

He made special note of those who usurped the power granted to Americans through their representatives. "Sadly, I have found that individual Members [of Congress], even though we represent our half-million constituents, are much less important than most of us would like to believe. The elite few who control the strings of power are the only ones who really count in the legislative process."

Paul has been noted for predicting several events, but one of his departing predictions would be proved false. "Thousands of men and women have come and gone here in our country's history, and except for the few, most go unnoticed and remain nameless in the pages of history, as I am sure I will."

Disenfranchised and frustrated, he left Congress.

Chapter 11

Ron Paul's hometown of Lake Jackson, Texas, was a vibrant yet peaceful place to live in the 1980s, not far from the Brazos River in Southeast Texas. The town began in 1940 as a planned community for employees of the Dow Chemical Company, and in the decade he spent in Congress, it had more than doubled in population, from nine thousand to twenty thousand residents, due to construction of a new petrochemical plant in the area.

The original town planner, Alden B. Dow (son of the founder of Dow Chemical), designed the layout of Lake Jackson. Alden did not settle for a square grid-system typical of city planners. Instead, he opted for scenic winding streets that coursed around the existing trees. Alden named the streets, usually ending with the word Way, such as Center Way and Winding Way. His whimsical nature was apparent by two streets that intersected: This Way and That Way.

Most members of the town had some connection to Dow—Paul's oldest son, Ronny, a graduate from the University of Texas, became a chemical engineer at the Dow plant and, in the summer of 1984, married Peggy Jane Walker, also a chemical engineer for Dow.

The people of Lake Jackson were stereotypically Texan: family-oriented, religious, warm and friendly. They enjoyed some of the highest per capita annual incomes in the country. Hard working and highly educated, many were doctors, lawyers, engineers, scientists and other professionals.

Not surprising for an area where summertime temperatures typically exceeded 100 degrees—often with 100 percent humidity—mosquitoes were found in abundance. Clute, a neighboring city, celebrated the insect with an annual mosquito festival.

The Dow Chemical Plant in Brazoria County

Back home at 101 Blossom Street, Paul pondered his mixed experiences in Washington and began planning for his future. "If there was a theme for the years 1984 to 1987 for Ron Paul," said Matthew Pyeatt, Paul's oldest grandchild, "it was reflection. It was an opportunity for him to sit back and reflect on his own views, and to deepen his views."

He was also returning to his chosen profession of medicine. Lifelong politics is certainly a goal for many who seek political office, but far from being resigned to going back to his day job, he welcomed it with relief. While serving in Congress, Dr. Paul kept his medical license current and occasionally practiced medicine when home.

His partner, Dr. Jack Pruitt, had kept the practice operating full time while he was in Washington, using the same offices Paul purchased when he first moved to Lake Jackson. During this interval, Pruitt abided by the two inflexible conditions on their partnership: no abortions and no federal funds.

Often working pro bono or accepting discounted payments from needy patients, Paul spent 50 or more hours per week providing medical services to expectant women and delivering babies. In the 1980s, the pager was state-of-the-art technology and Paul was among the first to own one, taking it everywhere so that his office could always reach him.

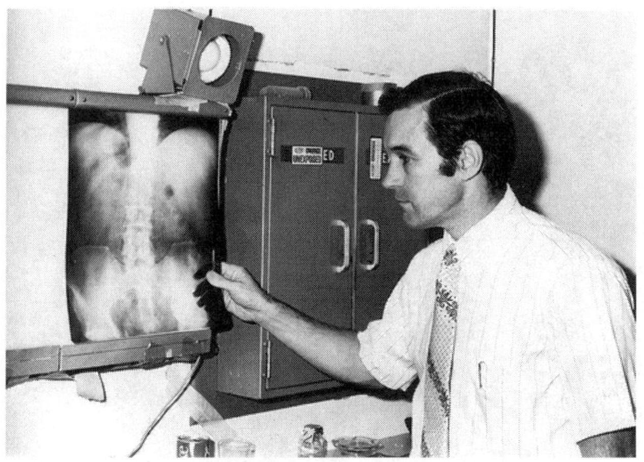

Dr. Paul back at his medical practice

Despite his commitment to the medical practice, he always found time for his growing family. Oldest daughter Lori gave the family a second grandchild in 1985. Paul's son Ronny married in the summer of 1984 and had a child, Laurie Jane Paul, in 1986. Paul was closely involved with both pregnancies, allowing Dr. Pruitt to oversee the births.

The Paul's third child, Rand, left Baylor University without a degree in 1984. He entered medical school at his father's alma mater, Duke University, to study ophthalmology (the eye and visual pathways). Duke accepted him without a degree due to his high scores on the Medical College Admission Test (MCAT).

Fourth child Robert graduated from high school in the spring of 1984 and continued his education at Hardin Simmons University in Abilene, Texas, joining the baseball team and majoring in biology.

With so much going on in his life, Paul still found time to relax.

He retained his love for swimming since his high school years—in the early 1980s he had an in-ground swimming pool built in his backyard, partly for himself and partly for entertaining the younger members of the family.

The Paul's backyard pool

The older members of the family had an on-going competition to see who would be the first into the pool at the beginning of each year and last to go in at the end of the year. The winner was invariably the one who could tolerate icy temperatures. Grandpa Paul usually won.

An avid cyclist, he would frequently ride for ten, fifteen, or even twenty miles at a time. He was a popular man in the Lake Jackson area, and those who saw him cycling would honk and wave at the friendly doctor and former congressman. As a keen gardener, he spent many hours raising organic tomatoes. All of these activities provided a contemplative environment to consider his future.

Paul left the US House of Representatives with no intention of returning to politics, but he did not see an end to his role as a truth-seeker and truth-speaker for the American people. While in

Congress he was forced to limit his association with the Foundation for Rational Economics and Education (FREE), due to its non-profit status, but without those constraints he could again speak through the foundation and actively work to develop it.

Over the next four years, he traveled frequently, talking to various groups about libertarian ideas. As founder and president of FREE, he routinely advised and warned Americans about the state of their government. During the early 1980s, at his home in Lake Jackson, he created his own phone service. He began taping weekly announcements on a variety of issues—usually monetary concerns and the continued growth of the federal government—that were available to anyone calling his phone number.

He also started a small-scale publishing enterprise, operated from offices in Nassau called Ron Paul & Associates. The new for-profit business produced the *Ron Paul Investment Newsletter* and his *Survival Report* to promote limited government and civil liberties. In 1984, the recently-founded Ludwig von Mises Institute published his fifth book, *Mises and Austrian Economics: A Personal View*.

Paul's time in the House of Representatives demonstrated to him that the Republican Party had lost its way on the issue of civil liberties. Early on, he hoped Ronald Reagan would bring about meaningful change, but instead the Reagan Revolution became a useful catch phrase rather than a real movement.

Reagan ran on a platform to dismantle the disastrous Department of Education, yet he was unable to achieve even this victory during his two terms in office. Partly this was because the Democrats controlled the House of Representatives at the time, but it was also a lack of will on the part of the Republican Party, who became distracted by other battles. Reagan's rhetoric about freedom was sadly detached from the reality he was creating. His passion for the War on Drugs made government even more intrusive, while his support of the gold standard had been entirely forgotten.

Paul would take his time away from politics to put his thoughts to paper, in the form of a book that would eventually go by the name *Freedom Under Siege*. Paul's former chief of staff Lew Rockwell contributed the foreword to the book.

Always a champion of the Constitution, Paul made individual liberty the flagship issue of his book. His introduction reflected his recent experiences in Washington:

> Two hundred years ago the United States Constitution was written as a guide for America's unique experiment in freedom. Today the free society that the Founders envisaged is barely identifiable. America is no longer a bastion of freedom. Prevailing ideology, grounded in economic ignorance and careless disregard for individual liberty, is nurtured by a multitude of self-serving, power-seeking politicians spouting platitudes of compassion for the poor who are created by their own philosophy. Reelection is paramount in the minds of most of those who represent us, while freedom and constitutional restraint of power are considered old-fashioned and unwise.

In the years following his early political career, he showed no concern for his legacy. He did not care what people in Washington thought of him and did little to maintain his congressional contacts or stay involved in party politics. He was instead content to stay true to his principles and continue to fight for a freer society, while working hard at the job he loved and continually renewing his commitment to his community as well as his growing family.

During this period, the holidays were especially important for the Paul family. With five children (youngest daughter Joy was still at home) and several grandchildren, the entire family would converge on the Pauls' home to celebrate Christmas or Thanksgiving. This included Carol's parents, Bill and Carol Wells.

Paul's retired parents, Margaret and Howard, would often join them from Pennsylvania. They had sold the dairy operation—along with the original homestead—when they retired in the early 1970s, about the time that home delivery of milk was ending.

Ron's siblings also occasionally visited. Older brother Bill was a mathematics professor, eventually becoming the head of the math department at Appalachian State University in Boone, North Carolina. David and Jerrold became ministers, and youngest brother Wayne became a certified public accountant.

The huge gatherings necessitated an expansion of the Paul family home to over 5,500 square feet. Ron added a bedroom and kitchenette to allow out-of-town guests to stay closer to family, including additional bathrooms to bring the total to five. He also added an office in order to accommodate his expanding collection of Austrian economics books. His office served as a quiet retreat in his ongoing study of economics, constitutional government, and individual freedom.

"Family was such a huge part of his life," explains grandson Matthew. "He was the patriarch of the family, but he was the quiet, lead-by-example type of patriarch, not rule-with-a-fist. He was a disciplinarian, but if you ever asked one of his children or grandchildren if they'd ever received corporal punishment they would laugh. He demanded that the kids do well in school and behave, but that all seemed to fall into place."

But while his family provided a refreshing refuge from Washington, they ended up paradoxically pushing him back into politics. He remembered his own upbringing, and his father's unprecedented freedom to build a life for himself and his family on his own terms. In contrast, he anguished that his own children might not have that same freedom. As his sons were now having sons of their own, Paul—by now in his early 50s—became more convinced of the dire need for a return to Constitutional principles.

He could do a lot as a private citizen from Lake Jackson, but in a country ruled by a distant federal government, which, to his mind, was sowing the seeds of its own destruction, something more than a newsletter was needed. In spending time with his family, he felt the urge to pass on the freedoms he grew up with to his grandchildren and future generations.

The only problem was, while he had gone far in politics, he had little interest in diving back into Republican Party politics and Washingtonian compromises. He wanted a national soapbox, but something radical, something that would afford him more freedom to say what really needed to be said. So, sitting at home, beeper on his belt, surrounded by his books on Austrian economics, and watching his grandchildren playing in their Lake Jackson retreat, he began considering his options.

Chapter 12

After three years away from Washington, enjoying his time with his family and working at his private medical practice, Ron Paul reentered the arena of national politics. Although he said in his 1984 farewell speech, "It's difficult for one who loves true liberty and utterly detests the power of the state to come to Washington for a period of time and not leave a true cynic," few who knew him expected he would stay silent forever.

What surprised people, however, was his decision to drop out of mainstream politics. On January 8, 1987, Paul sent a letter to Republican National Committee Chairman Frank Fahrenkopf announcing that he was leaving the party. He concluded the letter, "I therefore resign my membership in the Republican Party and enclose my membership card." It was not exactly a clear indication of his desire to return to national politics.

But for Paul, the move made perfect sense. He had found, in the Republican Party, not a natural home for idealistic dissenters, but rather an organization designed for careerist politicians. So, when contemplating a return to politics, he wanted a way to run for office on his own terms.

Immediately following his resignation from the Republican Party, Paul registered as a Libertarian. Shortly thereafter, he announced his intention to run for that party's presidential nomination.

The Libertarian Party had found uneven success in the 1980s. Still a very young organization, in 1980 the party nominated former

California gubernatorial candidate Ed Clark. Clark tried to appeal to liberals disaffected with Carter and with the increasingly heated rhetoric over Cold War foreign policy, coupled with a moderate economic conservatism that played off widespread dissatisfaction with the economic disasters that plagued 1970s America. He represented a moderate libertarianism, attempting to appeal directly to mainstream voters.

For his running mate, the Libertarian Party nominated billionaire industrialist David H. Koch, who pledged to largely finance the campaign with his personal fortune. This gave the duo a substantially larger operating budget than any Libertarian campaign before or since, and with it they were able to buy significant ad time on network television. The Clark campaign obtained ballot access in all 50 states, and ultimately pulled in just shy of a million votes; over 1% of the national electorate, a high-water mark for the Libertarian Party.

Four years later, after heated internal debates between supporters of ideological purity and those favoring mainstream acceptance, the Libertarian Party nominated attorney David P. Bergland, a longtime party insider, for the 1984 presidential campaign (along with Vice President nominee Jim Lewis). Bergland promised a return to core libertarian principles and an uncompromising ideological approach. His campaign, however, proved to be one of the least successful in the party's history, with just over 228,000 votes; less than one quarter of one percent of the electorate.

This left the Libertarian Party of 1987 pulled in two directions. There were many who were distrustful of compromising on core principles for the sake of mainstream political success, and there were others who argued that the Libertarian Party had to employ a big tent and reach out for Republican and Democratic votes.

Likewise, America at large found itself at a crossroads. Following the two terms of Ronald Reagan, conservatism remained on the ascent, although some questioned the Republican's ballooning deficits and substantial increase of the military-industrial complex. These were also the years when the Moral Majority had asserted itself within the GOP, to the continued chagrin of social liberals and moderate Republicans. The sitting Vice President, George H.W. Bush, was widely expected to run for Reagan's third term, but many openly questioned his commitment to conservative principles. The Democrats had no obvious successor to challenge him, eventually settling on Massachusetts Governor Michael Dukakis. Although Democrats had retaken Congress in 1986, they were still smarting over their crushing defeat in the Presidential race of 1984, among the most lopsided in history.

With these considerations, the Libertarian Party deliberated over whether to make a concerted push into electoral significance, or whether to stay true to core values and principles even at the cost of mainstream acceptance. It was into this divide that Ron Paul stepped.

As a former Republican and early Reagan supporter, many Libertarians had questions about Paul's desire to challenge the establishment that year. Addressing their questions in a speech on the campaign trail, Paul said, "I listened to Ronald Reagan in the '70s. He told me that he would balance the budget, cut back and get the government off my back. They are not off our backs, they are in our wallets and into our bedrooms and into our private lives more than ever before."

In the fall of 1987, Paul was not the only candidate running for the Libertarian Party nomination. Among the other candidates were Jim Lewis, a bookbindery representative from Old Saybrook, Connecticut and the former Vice Presidential nominee; Harry Glenn, a retired welder from St. John, Indiana; and Paul's chief competition, Native American activist and longtime Libertarian ally Russell Means.

Means, of the Lakota tribe, was one of the 20th century's most well-known leaders of the American Indian movement. He had taken part in the Indian occupation of Wounded Knee, South Dakota in 1973, and served a year in prison after being convicted of rioting and obstruction of justice. He was well known to the Libertarian Party as a committed freedom activist and instigator, and his political views were compatible with the mainstream Libertarian Party.

Russell Means at the 1987 Libertarian convention

Paul's campaign was in stark contrast to Means' effort. As one Libertarian participant at the time noted, "There was concern, at least among what I respectfully call the lunatic fringe of the Libertarian Party, that Paul more closely resembled a mainstream candidate. Here was a successful doctor wearing a suit, a total square, a professional politician, running against this other guy in a leather jacket. We were worried that the Libertarian Party was beginning to resemble Republicans and Democrats."

The conservative nature of both Paul and his campaign troubled many in the Libertarian Party. One of the most visible points of divergence was Paul's pro-life stance, with a legislative record to match. Pro-choice Libertarians, a critical caucus in the party, vigorously objected to his convictions and were only assuaged by assurances that he would not use his campaign to advance a pro-life agenda.

Another caucus with significant disagreements with Paul was the Libertarian Republican Organizing Committee, or LROC. LROC began in 1985, inspired in part by the more ideologically purist campaign of David Bergland, and took as its mission a push to resist the dilution of libertarian principles for the sake of more mainstream acceptance. Thus, their skepticism of Paul's candidacy was expected. Early in the race, LROC distributed pamphlets and newsletters outlining Paul's cultural conservatism and lack of adherence to an anti-state orthodoxy.

Despite this turbulence, the Libertarian Party eventually embraced Paul, in part because of his perceived ability to reach out beyond the ranks of doctrinal libertarians. As the New York Times noted on the day of the Libertarian Party convention, "The voting for the Presidential nomination appeared to be influenced by delegate desires to broaden the party's base. Mr. Means was seen as potentially opening an avenue to ethnic minorities, while Dr. Paul was seen as offering the candidacy of a trained, articulate political campaigner skilled at fund-raising."

Paul's run for the nomination proved unusually successful, and he won the majority on the first ballot. The final tally was 196 votes for Paul, 120 for Means, 49 for Jim Lewis, 3 for Harry Glenn, and 14 abstentions. Andre Marrou, who had recently served a two-year term in the Alaska Legislature as a Libertarian, was nominated as the Vice Presidential candidate without opposition.

After securing the nomination, the ticket of Paul/Marrou began campaigning in earnest. The first task was to build a staff, and Paul pulled from a number of sources to accomplish this. He had several experienced campaigners from his congressional career to choose from as well as the Libertarian Party, so he used a mix of both. Paul chose Nadia Hayes from his own ranks as chief campaign strategist. Hayes had worked for Paul starting in 1974 with his congressional campaigns, and by now she was a trusted advisor.

He also picked a number of allies from the Mises Institute and a few other outside sources. Burton Blumert, owner of the successful Camino Coin Company and friend of economist Murray Rothbard, would act as the treasurer and advisor to the campaign. Rothbard himself, who had been active with the Libertarian Party since 1978, put his full support behind Paul. Lew Rockwell would take on the duties of speech writer.

The Libertarian campaign seemed well organized from the word go. Paul himself soon proved to be exactly the "trained, articulate political campaigner" that the *New York Times* indicated the Libertarian Party hoped for.

One of their assurances to the Libertarian Party was that, given his political experience, he would prove an adept fundraiser—which would be required not just to attempt a mainstream breakout, but even to successfully petition to get on ballots. To meet his obligation, Paul found support from his former congressional colleague, Jesse Helms.

Burton Blumert, Lew Rockwell, David Gordon, and Murray Rothbard (L to R)

Helms, a former Democrat, was influential in Republican politics, although his fervent social conservatism made him a controversial figure. Helms was credited with rescuing Ronald Reagan's political career in 1976, resulting in a strong showing for Reagan that laid the groundwork for his successful 1980 presidential bid (Paul had also joined Helms as one of Reagan's four 1976 supporters in Congress). However, it was unlikely Helms could openly endorse someone from another political party, even Paul, without invoking hostility from Republicans.

The campaign was able to arrange a meeting with the Helms organization. Eric Dondero, who was Paul's travel secretary and "advance man" in 1988, describes the scene. "Ron and I went to meet Jesse Helms, but Helms was not able to attend. Instead we met with Carter Wren, a political operative in charge of Jesse Helms' fundraising operation. He hemmed and hawed. Helms didn't want to endorse Paul publicly. Wren let us know that Senator Helms supported Paul, but it could not be public."

Although no public support was forthcoming, the private support offered by Helms was even more valuable. "Wren shied away from public support by the Senator, but did assist with campaign strategy behind the scenes for a short while, mostly with fundraising."

The biggest boost to the campaign was done in secrecy. "We met in a dark backroom straight out of a movie," Dondero recalls. "Wren said 'We'll give you our top fundraiser,' and jotted a name on a pad with an address and phone number. Then we went back to Houston to give this gentleman a call."

The gentleman in question turned out to be a political fundraising powerhouse, David James. After an initial conversation, James flew to Houston to meet with the campaign team. In their very first meeting together, "Ron hired him on the spot," says Dondero. James would remain with Paul's organization for decades after the meeting.

The gift from Jesse Helms paid dividends as, under the stewardship of James, fundraising began to accelerate markedly. Estimates vary, but by October the campaign had raised over two million dollars, a healthy sum at the time for a third party challenger.

Ballot access was another early hurdle. Getting a candidate's name on the national ballot is nearly prohibitive for third party candidates. As Paul noted, "The laws are very biased, whether it's the Libertarian Party, or the Constitution Party, or the Green Party. It's very tough to compete. You don't gain credibility. You don't get into the debates. Even getting on ballots is tough." Ultimately, Paul was able to get on the ballot in 46 states, excepting North Carolina, West Virginia, Indiana and Missouri. Missouri in particular proved a contentious battle, and the fight between Libertarians and the Secretary of State's office spurred lawsuits that went all the way to federal appeals court.

Still, Paul quickly put himself in better shape than most of his predecessors in the Libertarian Party had ever managed. After overcoming these early hurdles, he was able to go about the business of taking his case to the American people. There was, however, the matter of getting that message to larger audiences.

Access to mainstream media channels was always a challenge for third party candidates, and though the Libertarian Party had been more successful than most in that regard (by virtue of their status as America's largest third party), it was still challenging to find avenues for getting the message out. At the time, cable television was not as popular as it would become and the Internet was jealously guarded by government institutions and universities. Although CNN was founded years earlier, the 24-hour news format was not yet ubiquitous. Thus, despite the fact that the former congressman had credibility as a viable political figure, national media appearances were hard to come by. "There was a major network blackout in the 1988 campaign," recalls Dondero.

However, Paul and his campaign had committed themselves to the philosophy that any opportunity to get the message out was valuable, so what little television time he was able to garner often came through appearances that more mainstream political candidates avoided. One notable appearance found him on the *Morton Downey Jr. Show*.

Morton Downey Jr. had become infamous as a loudmouthed, bullying host of radio and daytime television. His controversial television show, which ran for two years at the end of the 1980s, is often credited with popularizing trash TV. The discourse would often descend into shouting matches between Downey, his guests, and his audience. Downey styled himself as a right-wing populist, and appeared to take great relish in ambushing his guests and attempting to expose them as frauds or phonies (or, better still, instigating fights). Chain-smoking and aggressive, he took as his show's emblem a big mouth.

Paul appeared on the show on the Fourth of July. Downey introduced the candidate as "a man who could be snorting cocaine in the Oval Office." Appearing with a handful of other political activists, including New York Congressman Charles Rangel, it soon became apparent that Paul was the focus of the show, which was a barely concealed attempt at exposing him as a loon.

Paul appearing on the Morton Downey Jr. Show

If Downey and his audience expected an easy target, they had underestimated Paul, who refused to be shouted down. What followed was a riotous discussion of libertarian ideals, mainly regarding the war on drugs.

Paul also appeared on the long-running PBS show, *Firing Line* with conservative commentator William F. Buckley. Buckley considered himself a conservative libertarian and agreed with laissez-faire economics—if not on foreign policy. The one-hour episode, titled "The Libertarian Candidate", was an ideal venue for Paul to debate his political and economic ideas.

Despite these inroads, Paul's difficulties breaking into the mainstream only worsened as the general election continued into the late fall. One staffer at the time noted that national media coverage of the Libertarian Party campaign entirely dried up in the final leg of the race, as focus honed down to the "real" candidates—Bush and Dukakis. If Paul wanted to garner more than one million votes, he would need more exposure.

The campaign adopted a new strategy to court national media coverage, and responsibility fell to Nadia Hayes. The top of their wish list included network television and a front page article. According to Dondero, a large New York newspaper "promised Ron that if they bought a full page ad, the Libertarian Party would get a front page article. It was common practice back then to make these arrangements. The ad department called us about ten times per day, and they absolutely promised a front page article."

After a week of designing the ad and obtaining verbal assurances, the campaign went forward with the deal. "They took the bait and it cost something like $48,000, then they stopped returning her calls," says Dondero. "A week passed and there was no article."

The Paul campaign had made assurances to Libertarian supporters that, like the 1980 Clark/Koch ticket, they would be hitting the airwaves in October. But by the time October came, the promised media blitz had "largely failed to materialize."

There had been some promising signs. It seemed like media coverage was about to take off in October when PBS allotted Paul a half-hour segment on the popular *MacNeil/Lehrer NewsHour*. It was a big break for a third party candidate; the appearance garnered more exposure than he had received the entire campaign. "That was the highlight," says Dondero. "The MacNeil/Lehrer NewsHour was really popular at the time."

The campaign hoped other network news broadcasts would soon follow. But instead of taking off, an event at UCLA two weeks before election day proved emblematic. Paul was scheduled to speak with one of the largest crowds the campaign had seen so far, with hundreds of college students eager to listen to his message.

Before the event, Paul received word that he would finally have the televised news coverage the campaign had promised to donors. Campaign staff had received assurances, related by Hayes, that CBS and ABC News would be covering the rally. Before the event, a section in front of the stage was cleared to make room for TV cameras.

Paul waited backstage for the television vans to arrive as the throngs of students gathered. "We waited for one hour, but there were no TV stations. It was so devastating," recalls Dondero. The campaign team had no choice but to go ahead with his speech without any press.

"It was a wonderful event. I'm standing in the front, hearing all these students applauding," recalls Dondero. Paul delivered his message to the students, but the empty press section had turned an exuberant rally into a disappointment. "After the speech, he was looking at me and shaking his head. He wasn't blaming me. He spoke to a huge crowd! But that didn't matter to him. The only thing that mattered to him was the television coverage. … It was a huge disappointment for the donors."

As the Presidential race moved into the home stretch, Paul was largely passed over by the media. "We were very upset that there was no coverage. So much money went into it."

Unfortunately for Paul, things would only get worse. One week before the election, Burt Blumert discovered that over $100,000 was missing from Paul's investment newsletter account. Blumert and Lew Rockwell questioned the treasurer of the account, Nadia Hayes, and soon realized something was amiss. They went to Paul, asking him to level formal charges against Hayes.

Paul was understandably reluctant to file charges against his trusted advisor and wanted to give her a chance to explain the situation. Hayes' husband was in financial trouble due to a failing boat business, and despite Paul's confidence in her, it soon became clear that Hayes had been using campaign donations for her own personal use. Regrettably, Paul's efforts to obtain restitution and resolve the situation internally proved unsuccessful. It became clear that he had been betrayed by one of his most trusted supporters.

On November 7th, 1988, one day before the election, the dam burst. As *The American Libertarian* explained it, in "a bizarre twist, tough-talking campaign manager Nadia Hayes was sacked the day before the election. … Paul campaign chair Burt Blumert and Paul campaign ghostwriter and direct mail fundraiser Lew Rockwell showed up ... unannounced and unexpected [at HQ]. Staff were told that they should leave ... locksmiths turned up late in the day to change the locks on the office doors."

As the puzzled volunteers departed, Nadia Hayes' staff was escorted to a back room in the rented office by local police detectives from the Nassau Bay Police Department. As one staff member present at the time stated, "It was the most bizarre experience of my life. Here we were all set for an election party, busy trying to set up with state coordinators and state chairs, then they came in … and shuffled us into the back storeroom."

The campaign team remained in the backroom for almost six uncomfortable hours while lawyers, accountants, and police detectives searched through files in the main office. No one was allowed to leave the room, other than supervised breaks to the washroom, until all the evidence was collected. At the end of the ordeal, instead of the traditional last minute electoral push, the campaign office was closed and staff and volunteers were sent home. It was a crushing and disappointing end to the campaign, made worse by the fact that it was one of their own at the center of it.

At the conclusion of the investigation, campaign manager Nadia Hayes was arrested by the Nassau Bay, Texas Police Department. Paul later brought charges against her on March 23, 1989. His trusted lieutenant was later convicted by the Harris County Grand Jury of embezzlement of roughly $140,000, sentenced to six months in jail and ordered to pay restitution.

Paul ended his 1988 campaign as expected, in third place. The Paul/Marrou ticket received 431,499 votes, or almost half of one percent. Despite the harrowing final days, he received more votes than all other third-party candidates combined. His final showing was greater than the 1984 Libertarian Party result, though significantly worse than 1980. The Libertarian Party had strategically tried to split the difference between the 1980 and 1984 campaigns of Ed Clark and David Bergland, and had done exactly that with the votes.

It was no secret that the Paul campaign had hoped to exceed one million votes, and by that standard they had failed. But despite a last minute scandal, media blackout, and an untraditional campaign by mainstream (or Libertarian Party) standards, he was still able to pull in almost half a million votes and receive support from both conservatives and liberals, showing that libertarianism was not necessarily a niche ideology.

However, his campaign also illustrated the nearly insurmountable hurdles that any third party campaign must face. In that sense, he had failed to solve the riddle of breaking into the mainstream.

Paul himself remained unbowed throughout the election. "We live in a society where the only measurement is power and money," he said the week of the election, dismissing questions about his electoral relevance. "I happen to believe truth wins out in the end."

The legacy of the 1988 race was mixed. Following the embezzlement scandal, the Libertarian Party was rife with rumors, innuendo, and bad blood. This gave ammunition to elements within the party who were already unhappy with the ideological marriage between themselves and what they perceived as mainstream conservatism. In 1989, differences between the more libertine aspects of the party and the conservative wing flared when economist Murray Rothbard (supported by Rockwell and Blumert) failed in a bid for chairmanship of the party. Afterwards, Rothbard decried the failure of the Libertarian Party to transform "from a tiny social club for juvenile misfits and losers into a growing mass party of adults with regular jobs in the real world."

Heated words were exchanged between the promethean Lew Rockwell and Libertarian Party leadership. While Paul himself remained on good terms with all involved (later accepting an invitation to address the 1991 Libertarian Convention), in the end, Rockwell, Blumert, and Rothbard departed bitterly.

The Libertarians nominated Paul's 1988 running mate, Andre Marrou, in 1992, and running a more traditional Libertarian campaign, he only managed to pull in 291,627 votes (0.28% of the electorate).*

Dondero is even more direct. "In 1985, the Libertarian Party was near death—it was on life support," he states flatly. "[The Paul campaign] brought the Libertarian Party back from the brink of death, and gave it the kind of credibility it lacked."

Running mate Andre Marrou

And for Paul, it proved a seminal experience in dissenting against the establishment. The campaign represented his first foray into truly national politics, and the network he created that year, both in terms of donors and credibility as an instigating force for freedom, would prove valuable in the coming decade. Despite the tensions and dramas of the 1988 campaign, Paul's run for the Presidency that year marked him forever as a champion for liberty.

* The tensions and internal debate inherent in Paul's fight for the Libertarian Party nomination in 1988 would arise again in 2008, when another former Republican congressman, Bob Barr, would get the nomination on precisely the same promise of expanding mainstream appeal.

Chapter 13

With Republican George H. W. Bush declared the winner over Massachusetts governor Michael Dukakis, the smoke of the 1988 presidential race was beginning to clear. Ron Paul had some thinking and reassessing to do in regard to the direction of his career—and his life.

He had learned an important lesson in the 1988 race: although much good could be done outside the two-party system, the political deck was stacked against third parties.

"I probably invested close to a year," he told *Texas Monthly Magazine* in a later interview. "It was a lot of time and effort. Sometimes I had some ambivalence about how productive it was." In his typically polite manner, he understated the frustration he felt after the 1988 general election.

One thing he never doubted, however, was his passion for medicine. After the 1988 election ended, he naturally returned to his obstetrical practice in Lake Jackson. As before, his partner, Dr. Jack Pruett, had been diligently caring for their patients during the year-long Libertarian race. And, as before, even while engaged in politics, Paul had maintained a strong presence in his OB/GYN office.

Some elements of obstetrical practice in the early 1990s, however, stood in contrast to the way things were at the inception of his practice in 1968. Malpractice insurance premiums were rising and government Health Maintenance Organizations (HMOs) were becoming more and more involved in managing various aspects of patient care. Paul had prided himself on keeping his practice clear of government obstruction, but by the 1990s, it was nearly impossible to do so.

On his return, he noticed several changes, mostly due to the creeping influence of the Health Maintenance Act of 1973. "You had to call, and wait, and argue. They'd say, 'no, you've got to do this first. You've got to do the laparoscopy before you do the hysterectomy. You have to try this medication before you try that.' You'd do what they told you, and it doubled and tripled the costs. It just inflated them. It annoys the patients. It annoys the doctors. It's terrible. Managed care is just third party interference—another creation of government."

As he was apt to do, Paul also found a way to make a living by embracing his beliefs. He spoke passionately about hard money not only in Congressional buildings, but also at other venues around the country. Unbeknownst to him at the time, one of these speeches would lead him to enter into a successful business venture and lifelong friendship with Burton Blumert, dealer in precious metals and sole proprietor of Camino Coin Company.

Blumert had been a coin dealer since 1959, and had developed an excellent reputation within the trade. As such, he regularly attended events related to coins and precious metals. Naturally, he and Paul crossed paths in the early 1970s. "I met him at a coin convention," Blumert recalled. "He was speaking about gold and the [Vietnam] War. We had coffee together." That meeting was the beginning of, in Blumert's words, "a long and abiding friendship."

The two remained close in the years that followed. Blumert was affiliated with the Ludwig von Mises Institute, on whose board of directors Paul served. "He was loyal throughout," recalled Blumert. "He was there at every meeting that we had." He also chaired Paul's 1988 presidential bid.

Blumert saw an opportunity for both of them to combine their individual talents. He proposed a joint business venture, and the

Ron Paul Coin Company was formed. Camino Coin was the parent company, with Blumert as the sole proprietor. Paul brought his good name and reputation to the business (as well as his considerable fame among gold bugs), along with a diverse group of supporters he had amassed during his presidential campaign.

"You couldn't ask for a better name for the coin business," he said. "Ron had always been friendly to gold, historically and otherwise, so he was perfect for heading up the company. [...] We had become friends by that time. He knew and respected what we were doing, and to this day I'm very proud of that."[1]

During the decade-long business venture, Ron Paul Coin Company sold thousands of "Ron Paul Survival Kits." The kits were, as Blumert described them, "a big hit." They consisted of surplus ammunition cans from World War II filled with a mixture of coins. According to Blumert, there was "a silver kit for the fellow on a modest budget, and there was one with gold and silver for those who could afford it."

The kits contained US silver dollars and $20 gold coins, last minted in 1907. "Everyone who bought one of these survival kits," Blumert mused, "survived."

At that time, the late 1980s and early 1990s, Paul and his colleagues had expanded his in-house publishing business, now printing several newsletters—*The Ron Paul Investment Report*, *The Ron Paul Political Report*, and *The Ron Paul Survival Report*—which were mailed out to a list of subscribers. At the suggestion of Lew Rockwell, who edited the newsletters, the Ron Paul Coin Company included special offerings with some of the newsletters.

"Imagine having a city the size of Utica, New York as your client base," said Blumert. "They were very good clients, and very loyal." Blumert reportedly received offers from other coin dealers to buy the mailing list for hundreds of thousands of dollars. But, he said, "of course, we would never sell it. That's the way Ron is."

---

1 Blumert passed away in March 2009, shortly after this interview.

Although Paul enjoyed his association with the company, he was not in it for the money. He explained, "You only make five or ten dollars a coin so you've got to sell a lot of coins to get rich. I was just promoting something I believe in." Still, it was an additional source of income for the doctor, who prohibited his children from taking federal college loans, instead paying for their education himself. This, combined with the income from his obstetrical practice, allowed Ron and Carol to build a vacation home in the nearby town of Surfside Beach in 1990. Unknown to them at the time, this modest elevated home (most homes along Surfside Beach were built on stilts) would play a crucial role in Paul's future political career.

Surfside Beach

Paul's self-prescribed remedy for big government came in the form of freedom-oriented institutions. In addition to his Foundation for Rational Economics and Education (FREE), in 1989 he had established The National Endowment for Liberty (NEFL). NEFL was created for the purpose of producing television and video programs to advance the mission of FREE.

After the dismissal of Nadia Hayes, Jessie Helm's former campaign fundraiser David James took over her position within Paul's organization, which at this point was fairly ambiguous as he didn't hold an office. The Houston-Clear Lake office on Nasa Road One was used for the publication of Paul's several newsletters. With the arrival of David James, their activities took on a larger scope.

Due to their relative lack of media coverage during the 1988 Libertarian presidential run, Paul and his associates were eager to bypass the establishment media. The natural outlet for airing his views was through cable television, which was blossoming in the 1980s.

"David James' big project was a Ron Paul cable television series," explains Eric Dondero. "He had a dream of a libertarian television show nationwide that would air every Wednesday."

James worked on the television series from 1989 to 1991, acting as Executive Producer, with help from Jean McIvor. They modeled their production on the PBS series *The MacNeil/Lehrer NewsHour*, using funds raised by NEFL, with Paul as the chairman of the endowment fund.

James titled the show *At Issue*, and set out to create a weekly half-hour show with news items, interviews and panel discussions, hosted by Paul and moderator Mike Hayes. The show had multiple studio cameras, a quality news set, and professional editing.

Paul co-hosting At Issue

The half-hour show contained several segments mirroring *The MacNeil/Lehrer NewsHour*. The first segment featured a documentary report with on-site interviews with politicians and businessmen, background music, and even reenactments. The longer second segment featured an in-depth discussion of the issues at hand with a featured expert. Interspersed between segments were spots touting the show's sponsor, the National Endowment for Liberty.

James was diligent in producing the show, even going so far as to offer a preview of each episode to a focus group of Americans to gauge their reactions. Paul himself not only appeared on the show, but was also involved in the production.

At Issue was successful at attracting an interested audience. As the show became more popular, Dondero recalled that it even aired on some widely-viewed news networks. "They were good shows," he said. "Walter Williams was a guest, and Milton Friedman. They were well produced."

In 1991, after the show had covered the core libertarian issues, the series ended.

With the 1992 presidential election fast approaching and the lessons of 1988 still on their minds, Paul's closest friends and political strategists considered a second bid for the United States Presidency. They had been just as frustrated as Paul by the barriers to ballot access and media coverage for third parties. As Blumert said, "We felt that the experience we had in 1987 and 1988 indicated that a third party was not the way to run." Everyone decided that, should he ever run for president again, he would do so as a Republican.

Paul had opposed the Persian Gulf War from the outset, and felt strongly enough that he wanted to raise the issue publicly in the 1992 election. So, in 1991, his supporters formed an exploratory committee to challenge then-President George H. W. Bush in the Republican primary.

Burt Blumert was the chair of the committee. In October 1991, they began fundraising, collecting ten to twenty thousand dollars in the first few weeks, largely from readers of the newsletters and loyal patrons of their coin business.

However, during this time Patrick Buchanan, a senior Republican advisor to the Nixon, Ford, and Reagan administrations and political commentator, entered the race as a challenger to Bush. Many of Buchanan's positions were similar to Paul's, enough so that the campaign decided to set up a meeting. A private phone conversation between Paul and Buchanan followed. Because of Buchanan's anti-war stance, Paul was amenable to his ideas, so he stepped back from the race and let Buchanan take the reigns as the anti-war candidate.

Republican candidate Pat Buchanan

Paul was not altogether disappointed to drop out of the race. Blumert speculates that, privately, he was not ready to make that run, having been burned in the 1988 race.

They quickly found a home for the unused money that the exploratory committee had produced. As Blumert recalled, the funds they had at the time were "turned over to a PAC—America First Political Action Committee."

As the presidential races of 1988 and 1992 came and went, Paul had created for himself a potent political organization, filled with seasoned veterans. Ironically, he hadn't held an office for 10 years. But by 1995, almost inevitably, he made the decision to rectify that. He was once again ready to run for the United States House of Representatives.

As he geared up for what would be one of the toughest and most exciting elections of his career, he juggled campaigning and caring for his patients with his typical brand of finesse. "All through '95, getting ready for the '96 election, I probably campaigned for seven months," he said.

The 1990s were both a productive and an introspective time for Paul. However, he could never stay silent on the issues he saw plaguing America, at the root of which was an ever-expanding federal government. By the time the 1996 campaigns began to take shape, it was clear Dr. No was back.

Chapter 14

In 1995, the Republican Party promised a revolution, signing the Contract with America that included tax cuts, spending cuts, reigning in regulations, repealing unneeded laws, and dismantling entire unconstitutional federal agencies. Americans believed its sincerity and the Republican Party decisively captured both houses of Congress, winning a majority in the House of Representatives for the first time since 1952, when a teenaged Ron Paul was running track in high school.

To Paul, it seemed as if the GOP was finally set to embody his most deeply-held ideals of liberty. "I thought they might be serious about shrinking the size of government, which has always been my goal," he later recalled.

Paul had been out of Congress since 1984, but never far from politics in the intervening years. He had a following of over ten thousand enthusiastic libertarian supporters whom he had attracted from across the country during his earlier political career. This network of anti-tax, pro-Constitution, pro-free market activists would play an important role in what *The New York Times Magazine* later referred to as "one of the stranger Congressional elections of modern times."

Adding to Paul's reawakened interest in congressional politics was the fact that his home state of Texas seemed to be at the forefront of this new Republican Revolution.

Fiscal conservative Rep. Dick Armey of Texas's 26th District was elected House Majority Leader, while Paul's successor in the 22nd

District, Rep. Tom DeLay, was named Majority Whip (Armey's second-in-command).

Tax-cutting champion Rep. Bill Archer of the 7th District assumed the chairmanship of the powerful House Ways and Means Committee, which is responsible for writing federal tax legislation.

Sen. Kay Bailey Hutchison decisively won her first full term by a 30-point margin in a seat previously occupied by a Democrat.

And future president George W. Bush upended Democratic Gov. Ann Richards, thanks in part to his support of "concealed carry" legislation to allow licensed Texans to keep pistols hidden on their persons in public establishments for the purpose of self-defense, a bill which Richards vetoed.

Nationally, many other Democrats, including Speaker of the House Tom Foley, lost their seats to Republicans over their support for an ill-conceived "assault weapons" ban. President Clinton, who signed the ban into law, angrily blamed the NRA's efforts for the defeat of as many as 20 congressional Democrats. Responding to nationwide anxiety about crime, Clinton and the Democrats had critically underestimated the impact of the gun lobby.

The political winds had unmistakably shifted toward a desire for less government and more freedom. For 59-year-old Ron Paul, the time to re-enter politics seemed right. His partner in obstetrics, Jack Pruitt, was ready to dissolve their partnership, needing more time to look after his ill wife. And as ever, Paul's family, all true believers in the cause of liberty, were supportive of his decision to seek office.

Again he set his sights on the House of Representatives. However, he faced the prospect of winning over a soon-to-be redrawn district, different from the one he had represented in the 1970s and 1980s.

Paul thought it would be an unwise political move to run in his old district, the 22nd, against Tom DeLay, a powerful Republican member of the House. However, the new beach house, just twenty minutes away from Lake Jackson, was situated in the 14th congressional district. He recalled, "It was so close, and we were spending half our time down there anyway, so we just used that as the political address. That became my voting address. I ran from Surfside Beach in the 1990s."

His new 14th District was a sprawling, mostly rural area comprising 22 counties in the coastal region of Texas, lying just outside the large metropolitan areas of Houston, San Antonio, Austin, and Corpus Christi. Historically, it was a Democratic district, and the incumbent Democrat Paul would have to beat was Greg Laughlin. However, a strange political twist would soon change everything.

Paul reached out to DeLay to help him get in touch with Armey and the rest of the Republican delegation from Texas. Before announcing his candidacy, he hopped a jet to Washington, DC, with high hopes for a productive meeting. He assumed the Republicans would be interested in the possibility of using his candidacy to increase their number, perhaps offering him financial support and endorsements in his bid to defeat the Democrat.

"A court-ordered redistricting was coming up in Texas, and I told them, 'If you guys help protect my interests in this, I can gain this seat for you,'" he recalled.

The Texas Republicans were interested in increasing their number, but not in the way Paul assumed when he announced his candidacy to them. "I didn't think they were going to do what they did," he later noted.

What they did was follow newly installed Speaker of the House Newt Gingrich's strategy of boosting the Republican majority by convincing Democrats to switch parties. In this case, that meant courting the politically moderate Laughlin to join the Republican Party.

Laughlin would prove to be a willing convert. Before the Republican takeover of Congress, he was in line for a seat on the House Ways and Means Committee, a prized position that attracted large campaign donations from political action committees (PACs) and the Texas oil industry. If he switched parties, the Republican leadership, which now controlled committee assignments would make sure he got his Ways and Means spot. Laughlin became a Republican in June of 1995.

Democrat turned Republican Greg Laughlin

Paul was stunned. Now instead of running against a Democrat—one who had been bitterly attacked by the GOP leadership as a liberal in previous elections—he suddenly faced a primary battle with an incumbent Republican, with the support of the national and state party.

Another wrinkle was that rancher Jim Deats, who ran against Democrat Laughlin in 1994, had also entered the Republican primary fray. In essence, Paul would have to best the reigning Republican nominee, the incumbent, and whatever Democrat won that party's primary. What looked like a relatively straightforward race had suddenly turned into a massive uphill battle.

That was only the beginning. One by one, over the next few months, the leaders of the GOP establishment shunned Paul (and Deats), instead lining up behind Laughlin, who they thought was a safe bet. Their indifference toward Paul stemmed from a belief that he was not a team player. They believed his history with the Libertarian Party and disapproval of the War on Drugs would not appeal to mainstream Republican voters, particularly religious and socially conservative ones.

"My image was completely different in 1996 than in 1976," he later said of the campaign. "You can't just get passed off as an average Republican having done what I did. We got hit hard."

"Hard" proved to be an understatement. All told, Laughlin—who served in Operation Desert Storm in 1991 while still a member of congress—raised more than $1 million through the Texas and national Republican leadership, as well as from the PACs of 72

Republican members of Congress. By January 1996, Gingrich himself was campaigning in the 14th District for the newly minted Republican Laughlin. "I believe it's very important that Greg wins the primary," he said on a campaign stop. Other congressional Republicans, including Sen. Hutchison and Texas's senior senator, Phil Gramm, followed suit.

As a result, Paul found himself polling far behind, at 6 percent to Laughlin's 44 percent, but he remained determined. First, he reached out to friend and strategist Tom Lizardo, whom he had met in the 1980s. Despite the long odds, Lizardo moved to Texas to join the campaign.

Strategist Tom Lizardo

"He was the type of person who struck me very clearly as capable of taking an uphill battle and doing something with it," Lizardo recalled.

Paul also hired Eric Dondero, the former Young Republican who previously supported him in his 1988 Libertarian bid. Dondero moved from Florida to Texas in order to act as his campaign coordinator.

Daughter Lori Pyeatt and Carol Paul, both longtime board members of Paul & Associates, would campaign almost as hard as Paul himself.

And of course, he had David James, the chief officer of Ron Paul & Associates. James was a skilled fundraiser and Paul would need his abilities more than any other time in his political career.

James tapped into his national network of limited-government, pro-freedom supporters to out-fundraise Laughlin (*The Dallas Morning News* estimated more than 60 percent of Paul's campaign contributions came from outside Texas). Paul fought back by placing newspaper ads reminding voters that just 15 months earlier, when Laughlin was a Democrat, Gingrich had been slamming him as a "Clinton clone." The Paul campaign also sent out mailings reprinting a Republican attack from the same period that suggested Laughlin had taken illegal campaign contributions from a convicted criminal.

Paul's television spots also struck at Laughlin's reputation for taking trips abroad at the taxpayer's expense.

"We just had one little ad that we put on," Carol Paul recalled. "And it had one little man in an airplane, and it said, 'He went here,' and the airplane flies to one side of the screen, and then, 'he went here,' and then, 'he went here…'"

While the Republican establishment opposed Paul, he did enjoy one key endorsement: that of his friend and baseball Hall of Famer Nolan Ryan, a Lone Star State native who pitched for the Houston Astros and Texas Rangers, among other teams. Ryan served as his honorary campaign chair throughout the primary. Additional key endorsements came from publisher and tax activist Steve Forbes, and Pat Buchannan, returning Paul's favor of backing him in the 1992 race.

Perhaps most importantly, Paul remembered the value of personal contact with the people he hoped to represent in Washington. With the help of his family, he spent every day canvassing the district. His granddaughters wore red, white, and blue dresses, hand-sewn by Carol, which got the attention of potential voters.

"We would all fan out," Carol later explained. "Two of our granddaughters might go to a door, with one of their moms. And they'd say, 'I'm Laura and I'm Valori, and our granddad's walking in the neighborhood. Would you like to meet him? He's running for Congress.'"

When they met "granddad", many of them recognized Paul as the man who had delivered their babies. Strategist Tom Lizardo, then Paul's chief of staff, ultimately attributed the campaign's success to this personal connection.

The Laughlin campaign struck back by portraying Paul's Constitutional positions against federal involvement in drug prohibition as crazy, irresponsible, and un-Republican.

"They tried to paint me as a drug pusher," he later recalled. "But the voters weren't buying it. I had never advocated legalization and they knew it. I had condemned the federal war on drugs."

March 12, Primary Day, dawned bright and warm. Turnout was higher than expected, with more people voting as registered Republicans than as Democrats for the first time in Texas history. In the Republican primary, an outright majority was required to win the nomination—anything less would lead to a runoff between the top two finishers. When the polls closed, the Pauls patiently watched as the returns came in. Late into the evening, the final tally showed Laughlin with 42 percent of the record 34,000 ballots cast; Paul, 32 percent; and Deats, 24 percent.

Laughlin and his establishment backers were shocked that he did not receive more than 50 percent needed for an outright victory. They were further shocked when Deats—who felt just as mistreated by the Republican leadership as Paul—announced he was dropping out and endorsing Paul. A runoff election was scheduled in April between Laughlin and Paul to determine who would win the nomination.

The GOP establishment pulled out all the stops to ensure a Laughlin win in the runoff. The National Republican Congressional Committee provided Laughlin's campaign with support in the form of phone calls and mailings. Newly elected Gov. George W. Bush got involved, producing pro-Laughlin radio ads and declaring before an audience of hundreds in Laughlin's hometown, "The definition of welcome for this Governor is not only to say behind closed doors 'you are welcome,' but to say 'I have helped you win our party's nomination in any way I can.'" The governor's father, former president George H.W. Bush, also weighed in, endorsing Laughlin.

To combat the perception that Paul was not a true Republican, his campaign team produced a counter weapon—a video featuring past praise from Ronald Reagan. In response to the video, former Reagan attorney general Ed Meese flew to Texas to campaign against Paul, who, Meese reminded Republican voters, had been sharply critical of Reagan during his 1988 Libertarian presidential campaign. And despite Paul's support of the rights guaranteed under the Second Amendment, even the NRA campaigned against him.

With the entire might of the Republican establishment aligned against him, it appeared unlikely Paul would prevail. However, Texans have an independent streak and often rebel against being told what to do. When election night finally arrived, the results came in: 56% Paul, 44% Laughlin. The Republican efforts had been in vain, and the newly minted Republican nominee was now a candidate they had actively attempted to thwart, and who felt little loyalty to play by the party's rules.

Democrat Charles "Lefty" Morris

The Republican nomination in hand, the stage was now set for the general election in November against the Democratic nominee, Charles "Lefty" Morris. As bruising as the primary was, Paul knew he faced another serious challenge by Morris, a 56-year-old personal injury lawyer from Bee Cave who had the backing of the AFL-CIO, a major labor organization. Little did he know just how bitter the race against Morris—later labeled a "months-long hate campaign" by *The Austin Chronicle*—would become.

The national Republican leadership, so opposed to him in the primary, offered Paul no help in the general election.

"We thought we would qualify for a nice sum from the national Republican party—I think it's like $65,000 or $70,000—because they always reserve that amount of money for the nominee of the party," he said after the election. "But in this case, an exception was made and they spent it in the primary." In other words, the money the party usually reserved for Republican nominees had already been spent trying to drag Laughlin over the finish line, and the national Republicans had no intention of bending over backwards to assist the quirky former Libertarian who had just knocked out one of their highest profile converts. Paul was on his own.

The local Texas Republican Party, however, became more accommodating. "After Ron won the GOP nomination, mainline Republicans were unsure as to how to treat him," recalled Eric Dondero. "We reached out to the Bush people. After my conversations with [Bush advisor Karl] Rove, he put out the word to key Houston-area, Austin, and Victoria Republicans to back Ron Paul. All of a sudden, like a tidal wave, all the GOPers came on board our campaign."

For his part, Morris picked up where Laughlin left off. He immediately worked to publicize Paul's anti-drug-war views, characterizing them as absurd and out of touch. Then in May, Morris campaign staffers discovered a Canadian neo-Nazi website that linked to old issues of *The Ron Paul Survival Report*, under the heading of "Racialists and Freedom Fighters."

Despite the fact that Paul had no control over who linked to his newsletters, the media reaction was explosive. Newspapers across the state reprinted provocative passages from the newsletters, including a suggestion that former black Congresswoman Barbara Jordan was a "half-educated victimologist" and a supposition that "95 percent of the black males in [Washington, DC] are semi-criminal or entirely criminal." The Morris campaign heavily implied Paul was a racist and demanded that he release the entire contents of all his old newsletters for public examination. *The Dallas Morning News* picked up the story and the president of the Texas NAACP (National Association for the Advancement of Colored

People) denounced the newsletters and demanded an apology.

Publicly, Paul held his ground. Campaign coordinator Eric Dondero traded on his Jewish heritage, going so far as to wear a yarmulke to a press conference, and accused the Morris camp of ludicrously trying to paint Paul as a Nazi. Paul himself denied the charge of racism, saying, "I'm for freedom of speech, even for ugly things, but calling me a Nazi is the most aggravating, insulting thing that an opponent has ever done." (For his part, Morris asserted he never called Paul a Nazi.) Of the inflammatory content in some of his old newsletters, Paul said the "academic, tongue-in-cheek" writings were being taken out of context, even as he refused to release all his back issues. If people had questions about his character, he said, they could "come and talk to my neighbors."

Privately, Paul regretted the controversial content in his old newsletters. In an interview years later, he admitted, "I could never say this in the campaign, but those words weren't really written by me. It wasn't my language at all. Other people help me with my newsletter as I travel around. … They were never my words, but I had some moral responsibility for them." Who, precisely, had written the words in question would remain a closely guarded secret.

Throughout the long, sweltering Texas summer, the heated battle continued. Paul lost ground in the polls following the newsletter controversy, but thanks again to his large nationwide contributor base, he outraised Morris nearly three-to-one, garnering $1.2 million to Morris's $472,000. To help Morris, the AFL-CIO underwrote numerous anti-Paul ads, while the Paul campaign used its war chest to generate television and radio spots and mass mailings that portrayed Morris as a tool of shady lawyers' organizations and labor unions.

Cooler weather arrived with the November 1996 election day. Nationwide, voters received their first chance to express, via the ballot, their opinion of the Republican Revolution. They would also choose whether to give Senator Bob Dole of Kansas, who beat back an early primary challenge from conservative populist Pat Buchanan, the presidency and with it, Republican control of all three branches of the federal government—executive, legislative, and judicial.

The issues were much the same as they were in 1994, but the question of the Second Amendment and what it meant regarding citizen gun ownership also became a major topic nationally after April 19, 1995, when ex-military man Timothy McVeigh used a homemade bomb to destroy the Alfred P. Murrah federal building in Oklahoma City, killing 168 people. President Clinton seized on the tragedy to blame Republicans for stirring up hatred toward government and retroactively justify his "assault weapons" ban, even though assault weapons were not used in the attack.

As ever, candidate Paul came down on the side of the Constitution, agreeing in an issues survey to "Repeal all bans and measures that restrict law-abiding citizens from owning legally-obtained firearms."

Meanwhile, in the race for the 14th District, the last polls predicted a dead heat between Paul and Morris. In the words of *The Austin Chronicle*, it had been "a race that both sides admit has been unusually brutal." The Paul family waited through the day to learn if the agonizing seven-month campaign would result in victory. When all the votes were tallied, it was clear Paul was the winner with only 51 percent—a razor-thin margin. Morris was shocked and refused to concede defeat even well past midnight, when all the morning editions were going to press naming Paul the winner.

Nationally, the weak candidacy of Republican Bob Dole lost in a landslide to the incumbent President Clinton, winning only 40.7 percent of the popular vote, with independent Ross Perot bringing in 8.4 percent—an incredible result for a third party challenger. Congressional Republicans, thought to be vulnerable following the tragic Oklahoma City bombing, maintained convincing control of both houses.

The results in Texas's 14th District were just as undeniable. Paul and his message of strictly limited, Constitutional government would return to Washington after a 12-year absence, returning for the third time as a non-incumbent. And this time, despite a continuing Democratic presence in the White House, he believed real progress would finally be made to halt and even reverse the uncontrolled growth of the state.

With his political career reestablished, Paul felt it was time to close the medical practice. Dr. Pruitt's ill wife continued her convalescence and Pruitt required more time to spend with her. Paul himself would have little time away from Washington. After he was sworn in, the sixty-year old Congressman delivered his last baby and then retired from the medical profession. He would now dedicate the remainder of his career to politics—and soon become an even stronger force for freedom in Washington than he had been in the past.

Chapter 15

After a twelve year absence from Congress, Ron Paul was eager to renew his attack against big government. As with his previous terms, his role would be largely educational, both to the American public and hopefully to his fellow politicians. Although none of his colleagues suspected it at the time, his speeches to Congress would prove to be shockingly prophetic.

Paul carried over many of his campaign staff into his congressional staff. He hired Eric Dondero as a Senior Aide and District Representative, remaining in Brazoria County while the congressman worked in Washington. It was up to him to represent Paul to constituents—speaking for him, handling questions, scheduling his appearances, and dealing with local government representatives.

On January 3, the 105th session of Congress began. Paul planned to unleash a flurry of legislation on the House. He wasted little time making his return known. One of his first official acts was to urge every member to follow his lead in opting out of the lucrative congressional pension plan. Having refused to participate in what he considered an immoral system since his first term in 1976, he reaffirmed his decision as he began his 5th term in 1997, at the age of 61.

This wasn't the only measure he would take in an apparent crusade against his own Congressional interests. In February 1997, he voted for HJ Resolution 2, which proposed a Constitutional amendment to limit the number of terms for both House members and Senators. Like the pension plan, the absence of term limits created an incentive for elected officials to remain in office for life.

The existing system in Washington provided little incentive for Congressional members to return to the private sector. "Only when we limit the size of the federal government," he explained, "when we end the programs which allow for federal handouts, will we see our Congress returned to the citizen-legislature intended by the founders of this nation." Ultimately, the measure failed to receive the required two-thirds majority, although it did manage a 217 to 211 majority.

Although Paul favored term limits, he would not voluntarily limit his own terms because that would force him to desert the battle in Washington. To others, it seemed logical that if he supported term limits he would limit his own terms, just as he refused Medicare at his private medical practice. The apparent contradiction would one day come back to haunt him.

Before the end of his 5th term in Congress, Paul would also cast another vote which helped to solidify his reputation as The Taxpayer's Best Friend, this time against a Congressional pay-raise. "I have never and will never vote to increase Congress' pay," he said. "It's shameful that Congress seems to think that they should be raising their own pay at the same time the American people see their taxes increasing, federal spending going up, and the national debt getting larger."

His time out of Washington had likewise done nothing to soften his stance on monetary policy. He continued his vocal opposition to the Federal Reserve by joining two influential banking subcommittees: the Financial Institutions and Consumer Credit committee and the Domestic and International Monetary Policy committee. The former exercised jurisdiction over the actions of the Federal Reserve, while the latter monitored the results of the policies the Fed implemented. Always an outspoken critic, he now had an additional pulpit from which to hold the Federal Reserve accountable—and educate his fellow Congressmen.

He also continued to defend the constitutionally protected

rights of individual liberty and privacy. In April 1998, he introduced what could become the 28th Amendment to the US Constitution, HJR 116, known as the Liberty Amendment. The amendment, originally proposed in 1952, would prohibit the federal government from engaging in any activities not specifically authorized in the Constitution. The amendment would not only reinforce the ninth and tenth amendments, but also repeal the sixteenth amendment, which introduced the federal income tax.

While discussing the proposed 28th Amendment, he noted, "Over the years this amendment has enjoyed widespread support and has been introduced several times in the past by various members of Congress, but finally this measure has a chance of success given the conservative Congress and mood of the country in favor of a more limited, constitutional government which respects individual liberty."

Unfortunately, Paul's vision was rebuffed. The Republican Congress was not interested in legislation that it felt might hinder law enforcement. The Liberty Amendment went nowhere.

Later, he introduced a key piece of legislation, HR 4217, known as the Freedom and Privacy Restoration Act. It was drafted in response to the Department of Transportation's move to establish a national identification system. "Under the current state of the law, the citizens of states which have drivers' licenses that do not conform to the federal standards by October 1, 2000, will find themselves essentially stripped of their ability to participate in life as we know it," he explained. "On that date, Americans will not be able to get a job, open a bank account, apply for Social Security or Medicare, exercise their Second Amendment rights, or even take an airplane flight, unless they can produce a state-issued ID that conforms to the federal specifications."

His specialty, as usual, was to identify potential threats to the rights of American citizens by the federal government. He believed that the national ID was just another move toward cradle-to-grave oversight.

The defining issue of Paul's 5th term in Congress, however, was his stand on national sovereignty. He began to seriously question the interventionist policy that the US had been involved in for decades. On the House floor, he frequently voiced his opposition toward US policy, and specifically the role unelected, international organizations like NATO and the United Nations played in embroiling the United States in foreign conflicts.

Paul reminded Congress that, "George Washington, in his farewell address, told America to be weary of 'entangling alliances'. He understood very clearly what has since been either ignored or forgotten: foreign leaders will not do, nor can they be expected to do, what is best for American citizens. If we want what is best for this nation, Americans should be running America, not ceding rights and authority to international organizations."

With this in mind, in April 1997, Paul sponsored HR 1146, the American Sovereignty Restoration Act—the same bill he cosponsored with Larry McDonald years earlier. The legislation would end US participation in the United Nations. This included all UN military operations, an end to diplomatic immunity for UN envoys operating in the United States, and no UN access to federally-owned properties.

But while he waged war in Washington, Paul often found himself distracted by matters at home. His father, Howard, was not well. At 93 years of age, his heart was growing weaker and he was frequently in the hospital. Paul gave his father the best medical advice he could as a physician, but he could not halt the injustices of aging. On May 23, 1997, Howard Caspar Paul passed away.

It was hard to be sad about a man who had lived such a full life, and who had witnessed so much of his family's successes, including Ron's. The family flew to Pennsylvania for the funeral to console Ron's mother, Margaret. The time spent with family mourning the loss of their patriarch put the battles in Washington in perspective. All the committees, the bills, and the votes suddenly seemed petty by comparison.

After the funeral, he returned to Washington with a fresh perspective and a resolved determination to fight for what really mattered—life and liberty. He was understandably low-key for the first few weeks after his return, but he would not remain so for long.

At the time, the United States was meddling in the Bosnian conflict, known as the Wars of Yugoslav Succession. They began just prior to Bill Clinton's first term in office, when the southeastern European nation declared independence from Yugoslavia. This resulted in war between Bosnian Serbs, who wanted to remain part of Yugoslavia, and the Croats, who supported Bosnian independence.

Using the justification of UN support, Clinton deployed US troops to the region in January of 1996 with plans to get out within a year. Eighteen months passed, and Clinton now maintained that the troops would remain until June of 1998. Congressman Paul felt that this "peace mission" was beginning to resemble Korea, Vietnam, Somalia, and even the Persian Gulf War, which all resulted in more war and suffering.

In a speech given July 15, 1997, Paul argued that "not only has Congress failed in its responsibilities to restrain our adventurous presidents in pursuing war, spying, and imposing our will on other nations by installing leaders, and at times eliminating others, throughout the world these past 50 years, we now, by default, have allowed our foreign policy to be commandeered by international bodies like NATO and the United Nations."

He went on to address the complicity of Congress in continuing to fund an operation with no end in sight. "The recent two billion dollar additional funds in the supplemental appropriation bill were the cue to the president that the Congress will not act to stop the operation when under pressure to support the troops." In Paul's view, the best way for Congress to support the troops was to bring them home, rather than continuing to fund and escalate a conflict once the troops are engaged.

As was often the case, Paul found himself part of a very small minority, if not alone entirely, on many of these issues. As 1997 came to a close, it became apparent that the United States was headed for another foreign entanglement, this time in Iraq.

In November, Paul expressed his grave concerns. "We have been told by the Ambassador to the United Nations that the reason we must threaten force in this area is that Iraq is a direct threat to the United Nations." He added sarcastically, "Here all along, I thought I was here in Congress to protect the security of the United States."

In a personal letter, he urged President Clinton to avoid using military force in Iraq, since it would only worsen a situation brought on by decades of interventionist foreign policy. "The real problem for the United States is not Saddam Hussein, but rather our foreign policy," he wrote. "I hope your administration will mark a radical departure from others of this century, by following the advice of our Founding Fathers." Clinton was unmoved by the letter.

Paul continued to speak out against what seemed to be the inevitable—military force in the Middle East. He was critical not only of the ease with which the Clinton administration, and his fellow House members, seemed ready to go to war with Iraq, but the hypocrisy of the policy itself. Why Iraq? Why not China, or North Korea, or Russia? What were the underlying motives that led to singling out Iraq for their alleged possession of weapons of mass destruction, when the same could be said for any one of these other nations?

More importantly, why now? At the time, Clinton was embroiled in the embarrassing Monica Lewinsky scandal. News of an inappropriate relationship with the 22 year-old intern, and subsequent impeachment hearings, dominated newspapers and television media in 1998. The coincidental timing did not escape the attention of Paul.

On January 27, 1998, he addressed the House. "Mr. Speaker, it appears the administration is about to bomb Iraq. The stated reason is to force UN inspections of every inch of Iraq territory to rule out the existence of any weapons of mass destruction. The president's personal problems may influence the decision, but a flawed foreign policy is behind the effort."

He continued, "There was a time in our history that bombing foreign countries was considered an act of war, done only with the declaration by this Congress. Today, tragically, it is done at the whim of presidents and at the urging of congressional leaders without a vote, except maybe by the UN Security Council." He predicted that the US's role as the enforcer of UN policies would only serve to strengthen Hussein, unify the radical Islamic fundamentalists and increase the likelihood of terrorist attacks on American citizens.

Two days later, he gave what he called a "State of the Republic" address on the House floor in response to Clinton's State of the Union address. Again, he pointed out the influence of the United Nations on foreign policy, resulting in an erosion of US sovereignty.

"These days," he said, "not even the United States moves without permission from the UN Security Council. In checking with the US Air Force about the history of U-2 flights in Iraq, over Iraq, and in their current schedules, I was firmly told the Air Force was not in charge of these flights, the UN was."

On February 12, 1998, Paul introduced HR 3208 as a piece of emergency legislation. The bill was drafted to protect the troops and prevent Clinton from initiating the use of force in the Persian Gulf. The legislation prohibited Defense Department funds from being used for offensive actions against Iraq without Congress declaring war.

Paul commented, "It's horrible that our nation has reached a point where it takes legislation like this to force the President and the Congress to follow the Constitution, which is the supreme law of the land. I am disgusted by and opposed to any leader who uses lethal force and horrendous weapons against his own people; but until Hussein takes steps against the United States, it is up to the

Iraqis to determine what to do with him." He emphasized that he would have no part in any activity that would put an American soldier in harm's way to enforce UN resolutions, especially when there was no immediate threat to the United States.

After years in congress, the pattern was clear. Every time a tyrant was vanquished in one corner of the world, another one magically rose up in another, requiring US military involvement.

In March of 1998, Paul addressed the issue in the context of the continuing conflict in southeastern Europe, this time in Kosovo. "Mr. Speaker," he began "last week it was Saddam Hussein and the Iraqis. This week's Hitler is Slobodon Milosevic and the Serbs. Next week, who knows? Kim Jong-il and the North Koreans? Next year, who will it be, the Ayatollah and the Iranians? Every week we must find a foreign infidel to slay, and of course, keep the military industrial complex humming."

In the fall of 1998, the attention of Congress shifted again back to the Middle East and former-ally-turned-enemy, Saddam Hussein. The Iraq Liberation Act was passed 360-38 in the House. The Act was a Congressional statement of policy calling for regime change in Iraq. The stated reason for the Iraq Liberation Act was to "establish a program to support Democracy in Iraq." Primarily, this legislation moved forward based upon findings that Saddam Hussein had committed various violations of International Law, failed to comply with its obligations following the previous Gulf War, and had ignored UN resolutions.

Paul certainly did not see any of these reasons as a justification to declare "virtual war" on Iraq and give the President "tremendous powers to pursue war efforts against a sovereign nation." In his view, The Iraq Liberation Act amounted to a blank check written to the President to conduct war, off the books, in whatever manner he chose.

On October 5, one legislative day after the House passed the bill to the Senate, Paul addressed the House regarding the ramifications. Highlighting the unintended consequences of entangling alliances overseas, he pointed out that one of the reasons cited for supporting "regime change" was Iraq's invasion and use of chemical weapons on Iranian troops between 1980 and 1988. Paul agreed that the actions were worthy of condemnation, but highlighted that "the whole problem is we were Iraq's ally at the time, giving [Hussein] military assistance, giving him funds, and giving him technology for chemical weapons."

He continued, "Not too long ago, a few years back in the 1980s, in our effort to bring peace and democracy to the world, we assisted the freedom fighters of Afghanistan. In our infinite wisdom, we gave money, technology and training to Osama bin Laden." Paul was clearly wary of a coming tragedy if the US continued on its path of foreign intervention in the Middle East.

Despite his opposition, the act went on to pass unanimously in the Senate, and Clinton signed the bill into law on October 31, 1998. This set the stage for Operation Desert Fox, a four-day bombing campaign that ensued sixteen days later. Coincidentally, the campaign occurred at the same time the House of Representatives were conducting impeachment hearings against Clinton.

When Clinton eventually sent troops into Iraq on December 16th, 1998, Paul boldly called on the president to resign for the good of the country. "Once again President Clinton is using American troops to deflect attention from his record of lies, distortions, obstruction of justice and abuse of power," he said. "Even if one can look past the constitutional prohibition against the US policing the world, the timing of this new attack against Iraq screams of hypocrisy by a president who has shown a complete disregard for our military, our Constitution and our national defense."

"Iraq has been 'disobeying' the United Nations for years now, but suddenly, on the verge of his impeachment, this president decides to launch an attack, in essence an unconstitutional declaration of war."

Paul blasting President Clinton on C-SPAN

Paul accused Clinton, who avoided military service as a young man, of using American soldiers as a shield from impeachment. "How many American soldiers and innocent Iraqi children will die so that this president can hide from justice? How many American citizens are now at increased risk from terrorist attack because of this president? How much innocent blood will have to flow to cover this president's sins? This attack has no basis in protecting our national security and only increases the danger to our people."

As one of his last duties in his 5th Congressional term, Paul voted for all four articles of impeachment against Clinton. He observed, "There is a major irony in this impeachment proceeding. A lot has been said the last two months by members of the Judiciary Committee on both sides of the aisle regarding the Constitution and how it must be upheld. But if we are witnessing… a serious move toward obeying the constitutional restraints, I will anxiously look forward to the next session when 80 percent of our routine legislation will be voted down."

Ultimately, Paul felt that there were more serious crimes that should have been thoroughly investigated. "The fact that President Clinton will most likely escape removal from office I find less offensive than the Congress' and media's lack of interest in dealing with the serious charges of flagrant abuse of power, threatening political revenge, issuing unconstitutional executive orders, sacrificing US sovereignty to world government, bribery, and illegal acts of war, along with the routine flaunting of the constitutional restraints that were placed there to keep our federal government small and limited in scope."

Chapter 16

While the late 90s saw Ron Paul cementing his reputation as Dr. No, often as the lone voice of dissent, by 1997 there was also the matter of reelection. Like his hard-won but narrow victory in 1996, Paul's 1998 campaign proved difficult as well. For the first time, he had no Republican primary opponent to worry about. At some point, tired of expending resources to defeat him, and worried that he might bolt the party entirely if pushed too hard, the Republican Party leadership offered him a deal. He would agree to vote with the party on procedural matters (such as confirming nominees, organizing the majority, appointing a Speaker of the House), and in exchange the party would stop backing primary challengers against him.

But the Democrats, of course, had no such arrangements, and in Paul they saw a ripe target—a Republican so far outside the mainstream that he might be able to turn a red district blue. For the 1998 election, the Democrats nominated a seemingly formidable opponent in Loy Sneary, a rice farmer from Bay City and a former Matagorda County judge.

Paul's campaign team began by accusing Sneary of engineering a pay raise for himself and using increased taxes to fund a new wasteful government bureaucracy. One memorable campaign ad told voters to be "leery of Sneary."

This approach worked with voters. Ultimately, Paul raised $2.1 million for his campaign, compared with $734,000 by Sneary, a major factor in Paul's comfortable victory of 55% to 44%.

His sixth term started in January 1999, which included the last two years of Bill Clinton's presidency. Clinton had been impeached (but not removed from office) and was considered a lame-duck president.

Despite being in the majority party in the House, Paul continued to live up to his nickname, Dr. No. While voting with Republicans on procedural matters, he continued to vote against them more often than not on every other affair, and he had no compunction in taking to the House floor to call out what he saw as Republican hypocrisy on conservative values. He proved to be a constant and embarrassing thorn in the side of mainstream Republicanism—thankfully for party leadership, one relatively easy to ostracize and ignore.

One thorny issue was his stance on Social Security. Like the majority of the Republican caucus, he was distrustful both of the idea of Social Security; the government taking retirement planning out of the hands of citizens and putting it in the hands of bureaucrats. Although he opposed the Social Security system from both a moral and Constitutional standpoint, on January 6, 1999, almost immediately after being sworn in to his new term, he sponsored legislation to protect Social Security funds. As long as the federal government had a retirement program and payroll taxes were being collected for it, he reasoned that the funds ought to be set aside for the promises made to retirees.

His stance on congressional earmarks—a favorite whipping horse for House Republicans—was similarly incomprehensible to most of his caucus. Paul made a practice of railing against nearly all government spending. But when it came time to draw budgets, he would place as many earmarks in bills as anybody—and then he would promptly vote against the marked-up bill. His reasoning was that if Congress was going to steal money from his voters, he'd do everything in his power to stop the practice, but failing that, make sure that his constituents wouldn't lose out simply because some other districts' representative played the game better than him.

Some congressmen made a great show of railing against earmarks. Most quietly put in requests to benefit their districts. Paul managed to do both simultaneously.

While he was often a fly in the ointment for Republicans, at the very least he tended to set his sights on other targets. During the late 90s, the Clinton administration trumpeted how fiscally responsible the president was, taking credit for a balanced budget and federal surpluses. While the budget deficit was certainly less than in previous and subsequent years, mainly owing to the Dot-com bubble producing more tax revenues, Paul understood that the administration and Congress were using accounting tricks to make their claims of responsibility. On January 11, 1999, Paul wrote, "In recent years, President Clinton and Congress have claimed to produce a balanced budget. This balancing act has only come as a result of numerous accounting shenanigans, including taking money out of the Social Security Trust Fund. The trust fund has little actual money in it; it instead holds IOUs from the federal government, promising to eventually—someday, maybe—pay back the fund."

In order to build a coalition in support of the ideas of limited government, Paul helped form the Republican Liberty Caucus, a group of representatives interested in upholding constitutional principles. The group consisted of about 20 congressmen who met every Thursday for lunch to listen to guest speakers, such as former CIA analyst Michael Scheuer. Although Liberty Caucus members did not always vote in unison, they generally attempted to vote along constitutional lines.

Throughout 1999, Paul continued to sponsor and co-sponsor bills, including but not limited to, restoring Second Amendment rights, withdrawing from the United Nations, and enacting across-the-board tax cuts. By the end of the year, he had cosponsored a total of 200 bills in Congress. Although he favored ending the federal income tax, he still worked for tax relief in other ways, including supporting legislation to offer tax credits for seniors, educators, parents, and other groups.

In February 2000, Paul continued to support seniors by offering the Pharmaceutical Freedom Act, which was to assist seniors with prescription drug costs through tax credits. In April, he introduced the Cancer and Terminal Illness Patient Health Care Act, which would have waived Social Security taxes for individuals with a terminal illness. Although neither of these bills received additional support (as was the case with many of his bills), he would often propose legislation in an attempt to draw awareness to important issues.

In October 2000, he opposed the so-called "privatization" of Social Security, warning of the dangers of allowing the government to invest people's retirement funds in the stock market. He instead favored setting aside Social Security funds and allowing people to opt out of the system.

Throughout the year, he continued to question the wisdom of military intervention abroad. He doubted many of the government and media's claims about genocide in Kosovo. And on October 12, when the USS Cole was bombed while harbored in Yemen, claiming the lives of 17 sailors, he connected the dots between an interventionist foreign policy and the primary motive for the attack.

It was, however, Paul's continuing role on the House Committee on Financial Services (previously known as the House Committee on Banking and Currency) where he made the biggest impression in his second term back in Congress. The committee held little power, but serving on it gave Paul a fitting role as the often lone critic of fiat currency, the unstable Federal Reserve System, and Fed Chairman Alan Greenspan. Paul's role on the committee, the only one to which Greenspan generally reported, would create one of the most interesting rivalries in Congress.

Greenspan had assumed his chairmanship over a decade earlier, when Ronald Reagan appointed him to the post in 1987. He was influenced in his early career by Ayn Rand, the novelist who wrote the influential libertarian novel, *Atlas Shrugged.* Greenspan met Rand through his first wife, Joan Mitchell, who was friends with the wife of Nathaniel Branden, another noteworthy Rand associate. Greenspan remained friends with Rand until her death in 1982.

In many ways, Greenspan's chairmanship of an institution legally enabled to print money was at odds with his early career and his relationship with Rand. In 1966, for example, he wrote an essay entitled "Gold and Economic Freedom", published in Rand's book *Capitalism: The Unknown Ideal*, in which he unequivocally stated the moral case against fiat currency and for a monetary gold standard. He wrote, "In the absence of the gold standard, there is no way to protect savings from confiscation through inflation… This is the shabby secret of the welfare statists' tirades against gold. Deficit spending is simply a scheme for the 'hidden' confiscation of wealth. Gold stands in the way of this insidious process. It stands as a protector of property rights. If one grasps this, one has no difficulty in understanding the statists' antagonism toward the gold standard."

Fed Chairman Alan Greenspan

Because Greenspan's early writings were libertarian in nature, his career in politics, and his time as chairman of the Fed in particular, were viewed by many libertarians as a betrayal. Paul owned a signed copy of Greenspan's gold essay. When he requested the signature, Greenspan told him that he "wouldn't change a single word." However, in practice, Greenspan deviated widely from what he originally wrote.

Paul later noted his about-face on gold vs. fiat currency:

> I had an opportunity to ask him about his change of heart when he appeared before the House Financial Services committee last week. Although Mr. Greenspan is a master of evasion, he was surprisingly forthright in his responses to me. In short, he claimed he was wrong about his predictions of calamity for the fiat US dollar, that the Federal Reserve does a good job of essentially mimicking a gold standard, and that inflation is well under control. He even made the preposterous assertion that the Fed does not facilitate government expansion and deficit spending. In other words, he utterly repudiated the arguments he made 40 years ago. Yet this begs the question: If he was so wrong in the past, why should we listen to him now?

Starting in 1997, Paul had the opportunity to question the chairman twice a year until Greenspan retired in 2006. Paul believed that a currency, like any other good in a free market, could not and should not be centrally managed, planned, and controlled by a group of individuals. His questions reflected this belief.

While their relationship was congenial, their congressional exchanges were often not. On July 22, Paul suggested to Greenspan that he resign so as not to take the blame for economic problems to come. "My suggestion is, it is not so much that we should anticipate a problem, but the problem is already created by all of the inflation in the past twelve years and that we have generated this financial bubble worldwide and we have to anticipate that. When this comes back, we are going to have a big problem. We will have to deal with it. My big question is why would you want to stay around for this? It seems like I would get out while the getting is good."

Paul's prediction could not have been more accurate. On March 10, 2000, the NASDAQ stock exchange reached its peak and collapsed through the next few years, losing over 70% of its value. The S&P 500 and the Dow Jones Industrial Average would also decline significantly. This marked the popping of the "dot-com bubble" which grew under Clinton's reign.

In his sixth term, Paul sponsored legislation that called for the abolition of the Federal Reserve. He has also proposed other legislation through the years that would not directly call for the abolition of the Fed, but instead would either rein it in or severely limit it.

Paul's questioning of Greenspan was always interesting in that it did not follow the typical Washington script. In fact, he often seemed to be the only person not awed by Greenspan's reputation as the "Maestro" of money manipulation.

For example, he asked how much gold the US government had, as Fort Knox was not open for independent audits. He also inquired about the actions of the President's Working Group on Financial Markets (also known as the Plunge Protection Team). These issues were not general knowledge to his constituents, but he asked them anyway, not because he expected a good answer, but to draw attention to the government's secrecy.

Paul questioning the Fed Chairman

On July 25, 2000, Paul asked Greenspan, "Where do the Austrian economists go wrong? And where do you criticize them and say that we can't accept anything that they say?" Greenspan seemed to give an evasive answer, saying that many of the Austrians' theories are still right. His vague responses were typical of those holding the chairman position and he gained a reputation through the years of using "Fed-speak," or not being forthright in his answers and discussions. It was always a challenge for Paul to come up with questions that were difficult for Greenspan to evade.

On another occasion, he asked Greenspan if he thought that policymakers at the Fed wielded too much influence over the economy. Greenspan admitted "It is inevitable that the authority which is the producer of the money supply will have inordinate power." Although he seemed to be a thorn in Greenspan's side, there was perhaps a certain level of respect for each other as Paul always hoped that he was casting doubt in Greenspan's mind.

Aside from taking on the Fed, Paul's sixth term in Congress was full of political activity. Of course, the biggest political event in the year 2000 was the presidential election, the closest in history with Vice President Al Gore against Texas Governor George W. Bush.

Bush campaigned in 2000 for a more humble US foreign policy, explicitly arguing against the nation-building missions that characterized the Clinton administration (views that put him in line with Paul's own arguments during that period). Paul later said of Bush, "As a gentleman and as an individual, he's fine. I've talked to him quite a few times. I just think that his speeches were great in 2000 but he was misled by neoconservative advisors and he was overtaken."

As Bush lost the popular vote total to Gore, but won the presidency with electoral votes, Congressman Paul affirmed his support for the Electoral College and dismissed calls to change the system designed by the founders. He affirmed the fact that the US was supposed to be a constitutionally limited republic and not a democracy.

Congressman Paul's sixth term in the 106th Congress marked the end of the Clinton presidency. The Bush presidency would bring a whole new set of challenges. Now the Republicans would no longer take on the role of opposition party to the executive branch. Paul, of course, would be the exception.

Chapter 17

It was a cold day on January 28, 2000 as Ron Paul headed into his Congressional office in Washington, DC. In a few short days, he would celebrate his 47th anniversary with Carol. Today was the end of the first week of the 106th Congress' return to Washington after a holiday break. The National Oceanic and Atmospheric Administration alerted DC residents of a major snowstorm which had already dumped nearly a foot of snow in parts of Oklahoma and was rapidly heading northeast. It was expected to arrive by the following Sunday, bringing snow and ice to the already bleak federal city.

Later that afternoon, the 64-year-old grandfather would be speaking on the floor of the House of Representatives. He would try to derail a proposed expansion of OSHA powers to regulate home offices.

The same week, the Pentagon released the details of a failed ballistic missile defense system test. Seven years and $33 billion was all it cost Americans for the Defense Department to produce the non-working system.

In addition, the Clinton administration announced its intent to send $1.3 billion in foreign aid to Colombia, bringing the total to $1.6 billion over two years. Under the auspices of the War on Drugs, the expenditures would make Colombia the third largest recipient of foreign aid behind Israel and Egypt.

This was an election year. In addition to his Congressional duties and his plans to write *A Case for Defending America*, his tenth book, Paul would have to plan and execute a re-election campaign.

His Democratic opponent once again was Loy Sneary, whom Paul had defeated in 1998.

Paul's fourteenth district was enormous by any standard. It stretched from the coastal town of Surfside on its eastern edge, an outskirt of Houston, all the way to Johnson City, roughly 50 miles west of Austin, a span of almost 250 miles. From the south, the district began just north of Corpus Christi and reached to Georgetown, 20 miles north of downtown Austin, again almost 250 miles. The district swallowed up 22 Texas counties and contained three media markets.

In spite of this, he insisted on shaking hands and speaking in almost every corner of the district. Dragging family members and staffers along, he would routinely cover 300 miles in a single day.

There were no Republican challengers this year. According to senior aide Eric Dondero, ever since he reached out to the National Republican Party in 1995, they had left Paul alone and even helped his campaign financially. Thus, he had the luxury of planning for the general election rather than running two campaigns.

Having run against Sneary once before provided Paul with a clear advantage. But the Democratic National Committee was again, as it had in 1998, willing to spend as much money as necessary to unseat him. Fortunately he had fundraising powerhouse David James on his side.

Sneary's campaign strategists decided to attack Paul by painting him as "some sort of right wing monster." Dan Cobb, editor of the Victoria Advocate (a paper which routinely endorsed Paul's opponent), would later say, "It should be obvious by now that you can't attack him. All you can do is run a positive campaign. People in the Fourteenth [District] feel they know exactly where Paul stands. He is consistent and adheres to his principles. He has great personal integrity."

Sneary, the rice farmer from Bay City and a former Matagorda County judge, had high political designs. On June 9, 1999, Sneary testified in front of the House Committee on Agriculture, representing the US Rice Producers Association, to argue against economic sanctions on Iran. Ironically, this was a position shared by Paul. However, on most other issues, they were polar opposites.

As Cobb had noted, going negative against the incumbent candidate was a poor decision. Paul had a loyal following within his district, but he had also gained a reputation as a maverick outside his district and possessed a healthy mailing list. By this time, though most Internet connectivity was still via dial-up modem, his speeches and fundraising letters were regularly reposted to various Internet websites and news groups. The Libertarian Party, which was the first American political party to have a website, had long served as a catalog of Paul's positions and speeches. His strict Constitutional stance on gun control was well received in his district and his name became synonymous amongst members of the burgeoning patriot movement. And, given his popularity among "gold bugs", libertarians, pro-marijuana groups, and others, he had cobbled together a national following. The donations started pouring in from all over the country.

Sneary styled himself as a man of the people and drove around his district in a black Ford Bronco plastered with campaign signs. In spite of heavy Democratic National Committee backing, Sneary raised just over $1.1 million, half of that from political action committees and party officials, to Paul's $2.4 million. A whopping 93% percent of Paul's total came from individual donors, giving an average of forty dollars each. He was proving himself to be a true "man of the people."

When the returns finally came in, Paul improved over his previous margin with sixty percent of the vote. The results perplexed many observers, but to his constituents, there was nothing perplexing about it. Paul had won their trust and loyalty because his actions reflected his words. A month after the election, Congressman Paul's office announced, as it had done every year, it would return $50,000 to the US Treasury rather than spend it.

He was known as a retail politician, one who took time to meet with anybody from his district who showed up at his Washington office, appointment or otherwise. Tim Delaney, an editor for the *Victoria Advocate*, described his reason for continued electoral success as being very simple. "If a little old man calls up from the farm and says, 'I need a wheelchair,'" Delaney observed, "he'll get the damn wheelchair for him."

The New York Times Magazine, trying to figure out Paul's enduring popularity in his home district, noted:

> Paul may have refused on principle to accept Medicare when he practiced medicine. He may return a portion of his Congressional office budget every year. But his staff has the reputation of fighting doggedly to collect Social Security checks, passports, military decorations, immigrant-visa extensions and any emolument to which constituents are entitled by law. According to Jackie Gloor, who runs Paul's Victoria office: "So many times, people say to us, 'We don't like his vote.' But they trust his heart."

Paul was returning to Congress in a year in which the GOP had finally achieved the holy grail in American politics—a majority in both houses (though only by Vice President Dick Cheney's tie-breaker vote in the Senate) and a Republican President.

On January 3, 2001, Paul was sworn in for his seventh term as a Congressman. On the same day, he introduced a bill that would protect the identity of all Americans by changing the very nature of the Social Security number. It was obvious to him that requiring the number for identification purposes while also sharing it with private organizations was itself the root cause of identity theft.

His belief that the true purpose of government was to protect the rights of its citizens was made clear in his speech introducing the bill. Of this responsibility, he said, "I would remind my colleagues that in a constitutional republic the people are never asked to sacrifice their liberties to make the job of government officials a little bit easier. We are here to protect the freedom of the American people, not to make privacy invasion more efficient."

Not-so-gentle reminders of this sort were a constant during his tenure. He had not forgotten or ignored Congress' purpose as representatives of the people, and he would, to the chagrin of many of his colleagues on both sides of the aisle, remind them of this fact on every available occasion.

Though the Republican platform contained many planks to limit government power, and the newly elected Republican president promised an end to nation-building and deficits, Paul found President Bush wanting. One of the first flash points came with Bush's early proposal for faith-based initiatives–earmarking billions of dollars for use by religious organizations to provide welfare and education for those considered disadvantaged. It was sold as part of his campaign commitment to practice a "compassionate conservatism", in a framework that would appeal to his social conservative base.

The president, even prior to any Congressional approval, had created the Office of Faith Based and Community Initiatives via executive order, ostensibly to improve delivery of government services and remove barriers which typically prevented religious organizations from receiving federal funds for such purposes.

Of Bush's plan, Paul remarked during a June speech on the House floor, "Those who claim that the faith-based initiative merely saves charitable programs of religious organizations from discrimination miss the most basic point. The main reason faith-based programs are successful is the fact that free people choose to fund them and that free people choose to participate in them."

According to Paul, the true danger of such a scheme was that it would corrupt the very institutions which did so well without federal money. The organizations which received taxpayer funds to augment their work "may even change the religious character of their programs in order to avoid displeasing their new federal paymaster."

Paul addressing a near-empty House of Representatives

On July 10, 2001, Paul's mother "Peggy" passed away at the age of 93, the same age as her late husband had. She was an able woman who raised five successful children through often difficult times. Although both parents witnessed their son's success in politics, neither would see the full effect he would have on the American public.

Paul suffered from the loss of his mother, but an even greater loss was about to befall the nation. Back in January 2000, he laid out his statement of beliefs in a speech titled "A Republic, If You Can Keep It," based on the famous words of Benjamin Franklin. In it he made some startling predictions. Among them, he noted that Americans "are placed in greater danger because of our arrogant policy of bombing nations that do not submit to our wishes. This generates the hatred directed toward America, even if at times it seems suppressed, and exposes us to a greater threat of terrorism, since this is the only vehicle our victims can use to retaliate against a powerful military state. [...] The cost in terms of liberties lost and the unnecessary exposure to terrorism are difficult to determine, but in time it will become apparent to all of us that foreign interventionism is of no benefit to American citizens, but instead is a threat to our liberties."

As with most of his floor speeches, his stark warnings were largely ignored by his colleagues.

September 11, 2001 started out like any other day in Washington, but by the day's close, the mantra that America was now at war would be repeated by every media pundit, news anchor, and politician, save a select few.

Political sentiment immediately after the attacks on the World Trade Center complex in New York City was focused on revenge and military response. As early as September 13, the House had introduced a bill which would authorize the President to mobilize troops against the attackers, though there was not, as of yet, a clear enemy.

Paul was of the belief that such a response warranted more debate and consideration. Panic could lead to unnecessary killing and the loss of domestic liberties. There was a historical tendency for governments to ask citizens to give up their liberties under the guise of promised peace and security.

On September 12, Paul tried to diffuse a rush to judgment. He urged his colleagues to seek counsel from the Constitution:

> In our grief, we must remember our responsibilities. The Congress' foremost obligation in a constitutional republic is to preserve freedom and provide for national security. Yesterday our efforts to protect our homeland came up short. Our policies that led to that shortcoming must be re-evaluated and changed if found to be deficient. [...] When we retaliate for this horror we have suffered, we must be certain that only the guilty be punished. More killing of innocent civilians will only serve to flame the fires of war and further jeopardize our security.

This view, so early after the horrendous attacks, put him in a vanishing minority. The few liberals who took such a stance were roundly decried as being anti-American. Other nations who seemed similarly soft-footed were flogged in Washington and the press for surrendering. Bush famously decried "you're either with us, or against us." Paul, for his part, was roundly ignored as anachronistic in a time that called for stridency. Many assumed that his lack of full-throated support for the president was akin to electoral and political suicide.

Eventually, Paul did vote to authorize the use of military force in Afghanistan. However, he also offered alternative responses to 9/11 that would pass his standards of constitutional muster—specifically in utilizing Letters of Marquee and Reprisal—to no avail, and very little notice.

Beyond the actual military retaliation for the attacks, Congress also pushed forward legislation intended to shore up domestic readiness, the most infamous example of which was the US PATRIOT Act, which was handed to congress as HR 3108.

Paul was suspicious of the process by which the bill was handed to representatives. He noted, "My concerns are exacerbated by the fact that HR 3108 lacks many of the protections of civil liberties which the House Judiciary Committee worked to put into the version of the bill they considered. In fact, the process under which we are asked to consider this bill makes it nearly impossible to fulfill our constitutional responsibility to carefully consider measures which dramatically increase government's power."

Over his objections, the PATRIOT Act was passed and signed by President Bush. Paul was one of only three Republican House members who had voted against it.

On the eve of its signing, he spoke of the "sad state of affairs" in which the country had landed in the aftermath of the 9/11 attacks. It was clear that the current climate in Washington was enough to temper his usual optimism. Those who even remotely shared his views were being vilified in the press. He found it disturbing that people who were debating in good faith were being marginalized for political gain.

He told his House colleagues, "Throughout our early history, a policy of minding our own business and avoiding entangling alliances, as George Washington admonished, was more representative of American ideals than those we have pursued for the past fifty years. Some sincere Americans have suggested that our modern interventionist policy set the stage for the attacks of 9/11, and for this, they are condemned as being unpatriotic."

To Paul, the political response to the 9/11 attacks was one of the more worrisome events in his political career—perhaps more worrisome than the attacks themselves. The rush to provide remedies to government-caused problems was further growing government and expanding the powers of agencies he had been seeking to abolish since his first term in Congress. Those speaking out against the danger of overreaction were so few as to almost be non-existent, particularly within his party. President Bush quickly jettisoned the "humble foreign policy" he had proposed during his campaign in favor of something neoconservative writer Norman Podhoretz would later dub "World War Four."

By December, the Bush administration had already begun a press campaign linking Saddam Hussein to al-Qaeda. Congress was considering a joint resolution—House Joint Resolution 75 on December 19, 2001—to expand the war on terror into Iraq even before the first bombs had fallen in Afghanistan. Paul wondered aloud, "Is military action now the foreign policy of first resort for the United States?"

Chapter 18

Throughout 2002, Ron Paul continued speaking against Washington's drive to war with Iraq, pressing the case he had begun only days after 9/11. The Bush administration had taken an increasingly aggressive stance towards Saddam Hussein—a continuation of the Iraq Liberation Act which was signed into law by Bill Clinton. It was clear to Paul that the Council on Foreign Relations had more to do with foreign policy than either of the two parties.

"Both Parties are War Parties," he remarked. "Let's face it. That's what we have to admit. It seems that the Military Industrial Complex controls both the parties."

In August, the Senate Foreign Services Committee reviewed intelligence concerning Iraq's nuclear weapons capabilities. Paul feared that an invasion of Iraq was "a foregone conclusion," saying that the "testimony presented in the committee focused not on the wisdom of such an invasion, but rather only on how and when it should be done."

In September 2002, Paul delivered his case against invading Iraq on the floor of the House of Representatives. He believed that Iraq posed no threat to national security, calling the country an "impoverished third world nation 6,000 miles from our shores that doesn't even possess a navy or air force." He believed that the US military was overextended, and that invading Iraq would "dilute our ability to defend our country."

He further argued that the US should never go to war to enforce a United Nations resolution, and that it should never attack another country without a clear congressional declaration. He predicted that invading Iraq would wreak havoc on an already shaky US economy and ultimately hurt Republicans politically.

From a broader philosophical perspective, he opposed the war because of the growth of government and loss of liberty he believed would occur, noting that "many of the worst government programs of the 20th century began during wartime 'emergencies' and were never abolished."

Predictably, his House colleagues ignored his warnings. On October 10, Congress passed a resolution giving President Bush the authority to wage war in Iraq at his discretion. Paul was one of only six House Republicans to vote against the resolution. He was irate at his colleagues' shirking of their Constitutional responsibility to declare war, accusing them of "lack[ing] the political courage to call an invasion of Iraq what it really is: a war."

In late 2002, Paul faced re-election—his first after vocally opposing the president's reaction to 9/11. Even though he had spoken out against fellow Texan George W. Bush, the Republican leadership honored its previous agreement with Paul and did not back an opposing candidate.

After winning the uncontested Republican primary, he faced off against Democratic challenger Corby Windham, a 33-year old bilingual lawyer, former soldier, and former teacher from San Marcos. On November 22, Paul held his congressional seat convincingly with 102,661 votes to 48,192.

Less than a week after securing his spot in the 108th Congress, the UN Security Council passed a US-backed resolution demanding that Saddam Hussein allow weapons inspectors into Iraq or "face serious consequences."

Hussein immediately agreed to comply with the resolution, inviting UN weapons inspectors into Baghdad. On December 7, Iraq issued a 12,000-page report on its weapons programs to inspectors. Within days, the US and UK accused Iraq of not declaring a full and complete report of its weapons programs. Chief UN weapons inspector Hans Blix said that pieces were missing from the report, but felt that progress was being made. US ambassador to the UN John Negroponte disagreed with Blix's assessment, saying that Iraq had "spurned its last opportunity to comply with its disarmament obligations."

As the Bush administration's war rhetoric grew more confrontational, Paul continued to protest an invasion in weekly columns posted on his House website and in speeches on the House floor. In one speech, he listed the possible negative outcomes of war. He predicted that if the US were to invade Iraq, "al-Qaeda likely [would] get a real boost in membership." He listed the problems associated with rebuilding a post-war Iraq and choosing leadership among Iraq's three major ethnic factions: Sunnis, Shi'ites, and Kurds. "Do we really believe that somehow we can choose the 'good guys' who deserve to rule Iraq?" he asked. He reminded the Republican Party of its previous positions against nation-building which is what, he argued, having the US military descend on Iraq would entail.

On February 5, 2003, Secretary of State Colin Powell spoke to the UN Security Council, presenting evidence for the existence of illegal weapons in Iraq. Powell demanded that the Security Council come down aggressively against Iraq's violations of the 1991 cease-fire agreement it had signed following the first Gulf War.

Two Security Council members, France and Russia, continued to express reservations about authorizing an invasion. The UN hesitance to support regime change in Iraq frustrated the Bush administration, who began to entertain the possibility of invading unilaterally.

Paul was irritated by the mixed signals from the Bush administration regarding the UN. He felt that if the US was willing to invade Iraq on its own, asking for UN approval in the first place was unnecessary. "The bizarre irony is while we may act unilaterally in Iraq, the very justification for our invasion is that we are enforcing UN resolutions," he said.

On March 7, 2003, in a last-ditch effort to secure UN support for an invasion, the US presented the Security Council with a resolution demanding that Saddam Hussein disarm within ten days or face war. France and Russia vetoed the measure. By March 17, Iraq had apparently not met those demands, and the US, along with its pro-war allies Spain and Britain, abandoned efforts to seek UN approval to invade. Instead they insisted that previous UN resolutions gave them the authority. The message from Washington seemed to declare war was imminent.

The war began on March 19, as the US-led coalition launched Operation Iraqi Freedom. Within six weeks, coalition forces defeated Hussein's Republican Guard and took control of every major Iraqi city. On May 1, 2003, President Bush stood on the USS Abraham Lincoln in front of a banner that read, "Mission Accomplished" and declared an end to major combat operations in Iraq.

In the months following the ceremony, Iraqi rebels continued to kill and maim US troops in large numbers. Furthermore, coalition forces were unable to find the weapons of mass destruction (WMD) that the Bush administration had cited as justification for war. The President's approval ratings began to sink.

In June, several high ranking military officials predicted that rebuilding Iraq would cost the US hundreds of billions of dollars and require years of occupation. Paul feared that a long and costly nation building campaign in Iraq would drain Americans of their wealth and damage the economy.

He was disappointed in his Republican Party colleagues, who during Clinton's Presidency had carried the banner of non-intervention in foreign affairs. They now endorsed an occupation of Iraq that threatened to claim thousands of lives and drain hundreds of billions of dollars from US taxpayers.

On July 10, 2003, in an impassioned speech on the House floor,

Paul declared that the limited government movement in the US was dead. "There has not been, nor will there soon be, a conservative revolution in Washington," he said. It was one more disappointment following the squandered opportunity to shrink the size of government after Republicans had won control of Congress back in 1994.

Paul blamed this failure on the rise of neoconservatism within the Republican Party. Neoconservatives, he said, weren't conservatives at all, but rather big government liberals who favored using military force to impose the American way of life on the rest of the world. He feared that if the neoconservatives continued to control the Republican Party, "limiting the size and scope of government will be a long-forgotten dream."

In the middle of 2003, Paul had a falling out with his longtime senior aide, Eric Dondero. According to Dondero, the break was directly caused by their differences on foreign policy. "Ron Paul and I agree on about 95% of all domestic issues," he later wrote. "We disagree on a myriad of foreign policy and defense issues."

Dondero was a heavyset former military man, having served four years in the United States Navy. In contrast to the reserved, polite disposition of Paul, Dondero was outspoken, boisterous, and sometimes even crude. He would always speak his mind—a quality Paul respected. He was proudly Jewish and proudly Italian-American, occasionally signing his name Eric Dondero Rittberg.

Paul's former aide Eric Dondero

When the neoconservatives began pushing for war with Iraq, the split between Paul and Dondero widened. Saddam Hussein, an ally of the US in the 1980s, became an enemy to the Israeli cause when he announced his support for the Palestinians. Dondero believed the war with Iraq was justified.

In the summer of 2003, Paul asked Dondero to accompany

him on a ride to an event in Victoria, Texas, a two and a half hour drive from Lake Jackson. He wanted to discuss foreign policy, but Dondero remained aloof and evasive for most of the trip.

When they finally reached Victoria, Dondero released his pent up thoughts, heatedly telling his employer he thought he was wrong on the Iraq War. Paul, bristling with emotion himself, replied, "I will have nobody working for me on my staff who supports the War in Iraq—even you."

For the next six months, neither man spoke to one another. Dondero virtually ceased work for Paul, although he remained on the payroll until 2004. According to Dondero, "Finally, Chief of Staff Tom Lizardo suggested that Ron and I not talking to each other was not helpful to the 'atmosphere' in the District offices. I offered to my friend Tom to resign. We discussed a date, two months out, and a compensation package and I agreed."

In February 2004, Paul gave a speech to his House colleagues criticizing the US policy of promoting democracy abroad with military force. For all the talk of building a democratic Iraq, he claimed the US seemed averse to democracy when it didn't suit its own interests. He noted the US government's hesitance to allow Iraq to hold free elections, suggesting that it feared a "national election in Iraq would bring individuals to power that the administration doesn't want." Paul offered an alternative solution: the US could promote democracy "through persuasion and example."

On the one-year anniversary of the Iraq invasion, Paul reiterated his opposition to the war and questioned whether the war had improved the situation. "The young men and women who were hurt or killed certainly are no better off. Their families are no better off. Taxpayers are no better off," he said. If sacrificing American lives to save a nation from one cruel dictator was justified, Paul wondered how many American lives should be sacrificed to free people from other oppressive governments throughout the world.

While his initial objections to America's responses to 9/11 made him even more of a pariah than he had ever been, particularly within his own party, by 2004 popularity for the war was in rapid decline. Some Democratic politicians began taking the first tentative steps towards opposing the dominant view. Once Howard Dean, former governor of Vermont, began actively criticizing the War in Iraq and PATRIOT Act in the Democratic primaries for President—and quickly became a frontrunner because of it—opinion seemed to turn. Politicians who had previously supported the war became critics.

Paul was happy for the company, but somewhat annoyed at the fair-weather nature of these new war critics. If the war had been an unbridled success, he reasoned, all politicians who had voted for it would boast about their support. As it turned out, the military struggled to secure peace in Iraq, and found no WMD. The reversal was not unnoticed by Paul. "Some of today's critics were strongly in favor of going to war against Iraq when doing so appeared politically popular, but now are chagrined that the war is not going as smoothly as was hoped," he noted. He was one of a few who had opposed the war from the start, not because he thought it would fail, but because of true principles.

One of Paul's biggest fears was that the US invasion of Iraq would lead to meddling elsewhere. In May 2004, the House considered legislation that threatened to "use all appropriate means to deter, dissuade, and prevent Iran from acquiring nuclear weapons." Paul was disappointed that, in spite of the failure in Iraq, his colleagues were acting aggressively towards another Middle Eastern nation. He argued that the legislation, which called for strict economic sanctions against Iran, would do little to dissuade Iranian president Mahmoud Ahmadinejad from developing nuclear weapons. It would instead "sow misery among the poorest and most vulnerable segments" of Iran's population.

In December, a Pentagon study revealed the Iraq war had sparked an increase in terrorism in the Middle East. The war that had cost the US billions of dollars and thousands of lives was doing precisely the opposite of its alleged goals, as Paul had predicted back in 2002.

As his term came to a close, Paul weighed in on the approaching Presidential election. Without mentioning him by name, Paul chastised Democratic candidate John Kerry's frequent talk of a "plan" for America. He wrote that "government is not supposed to plan our lives or run the country; we are supposed to be free," arguing that centrally-planned economies always lead to low standards of living.

Though at odds with Republicans on foreign policy during his seventh term, he didn't completely break ranks with his party, instead siding with them on a number of fiscal issues. He joined Republicans in support of the President's proposal to cut double taxation of dividends. He also spoke in favor of Bush's Tax-Free Savings Plan, arguing that the plan "could put millions of Americans on the road to self-sufficiency."

However, he strongly opposed a Republican-supported Medicare prescription drug measure, believing the bill should never have been backed by anyone claiming to be a fiscal conservative. He said the bill was consistent with the "New Deal and Great Society programs of the utopian left" and would leave "true conservatives … wondering whether they still have a political home in the modern GOP."

Chapter 19

By 2004, Ron Paul had fought his battle for decades, yet it seemed like the United States was no closer to the free society envisioned by its founders. In light of this, he decided to seek another term in congress. This would be his first election since 1988 without his campaign coordinator, Eric Dondero, by his side. Fortunately he would not require a campaign team this time around. In the upcoming 2004 general election, which would be held on November 2 (concurrent with the presidential election), he faced no opposition—from Republicans or Democrats.

He was the only Texan from either party who ran unopposed and one of only 17 Republicans nationwide without a competitor. There were many possible reasons why no Democrat chose to run against him—after all, Texas' 14th district had mostly been a Democratic stronghold in the past. The most important was that, on a tactical level, Paul had beaten his Democratic opponent by increasing margins: 55% in 1998, then by 60% and finally with 68%. Thus his seat was seen as entrenched by the opposing party. Paul was naturally happy to continue his congressional work unopposed, and he saw an opportunity to address one particular issue that had been plaguing him for some time.

After Congress adjourned in October 2004, Paul took drastic measures to relieve his chronic knee pain. The injury he had suffered while playing football in high school finally came to a critical juncture. He was physically active even compared to men half his age, but years of wear to his damaged knee finally caught up with him, and his knees began feeling weak. Although biking didn't cause any problems, he was feeling pain while standing in the House of Representatives and walking to and from his office.

Paul was relieved he would not have to walk door-to-door campaigning in all four corners of his large district. When he realized he was unopposed, he and his doctor scheduled a surgery—and ensuing recovery time—so it would not interfere with his political duties. In October, he had both his knee joints surgically removed and replaced with artificial joints composed of titanium and plastic.

Post surgery, he spent less than a week in the hospital before rolling out in a wheel chair. For the next three weeks the housebound doctor limped around on crutches, often braving cooler temperatures in the swimming pool to help rehabilitate his knees and maintain joint mobility.

Eventually he was able to put his full weight on his new knees and he switched to limping about with a cane. By the end of the year, he was fully healed and walking without aid, in time for his next term in congress. He would need his new knees if he wanted to continue standing on the House floor delivering speeches in support of freedom.

The 109th United States Congress, Paul's ninth full term, began on January 3, 2005. The Senate consisted of 55 Republicans, 44 Democrats and one independent from Vermont, while the House of Representatives had 232 Republicans, 201 Democrats and one independent, again from Vermont. As George W. Bush had won the November election against Democrat John Kerry, it meant that the Republicans now dominated all three branches of the Federal Government. Despite the fact that Paul's repeated assertions that the Republican Party was the natural home for non-interventionism, both in foreign engagements and in domestic ones, he had no reason to believe that the new Republican majorities would bring an increase in support for a liberty agenda, as he defined it.

In early 2005, housing prices had peaked and it appeared an economic bubble was about to burst. Paul gave an interview to the *New York Times* and vowed, "We will go back to the gold standard, even if it takes the near-destruction of the dollar to get there." This was not a threat, but a prediction, just as his repeated assertions that, according to Ludwig von Mises and other Austrian economists, the American economy would soon go through a violent contraction.

In the 109th Congressional session the most important issues were the growing opposition against the Iraq war, the Hurricane Katrina disaster and immigration reform.

The immigration issue continued to intensify due to ongoing concerns in the aftermath of 9/11. Many Americans, fearful of terrorists crossing into the United States and undertaking more attacks, desired a tighter border. The immigration issue was further bolstered by a general anxiety of illegal immigrants taking American jobs, increasing crime and pushing down wages. By 2004, estimates of illegal immigrants in the United States ranged from eight to twelve million.

Lou Dobbs of CNN, the mild mannered host of *Moneyline*, was one of the first commentators to take up the issue seriously. The immigration issue gained an even larger platform in 2005 when a group calling themselves The Minuteman Project began patrolling the US-Mexican border. These were private citizens who were disappointed with their government's lack of effectiveness in keeping out illegal immigrants, so they took matters into their own hands.

Minuteman Project volunteers watching the border

Paul's views on illegal immigration differed significantly from when he ran as a Libertarian in 1988. During his previous presidential run, he took the classic Libertarian position, stating, "As in our country's first 150 years, there shouldn't be any immigration policy at all. We should welcome everyone who wants to come here and work."

After the election, both Paul's views and even those of libertarians began to shift. In the welfare-warfare political culture of 2005, Paul supported conditional free immigration. According to Paul:

> The immigration problem fundamentally is a welfare state problem. It is not anti-immigrant. Some illegal immigrants—certainly not all—receive housing subsidies, food stamps, free medical care, and other forms of welfare. This alienates taxpayers and breeds suspicion of immigrants, even though the majority of them work very hard. Without a welfare state, we would know that everyone coming to America wanted to work hard and support himself. Since we have accepted a permanent welfare state, however, we cannot be surprised when some freeloaders and criminals are attracted to our shores. Welfare muddies the question of why immigrants want to come here.

The first immigration related bill of the 109th Congress was HR 418, also known as the Real ID Act of 2005. It was sold as a way of separating law-abiding Americans from illegals. Paul saw it differently. On February 9, he delivered a speech titled "A National ID Bill Masquerading as Immigration Reform." The House was quite empty when the House speaker gave him permission to deliver his message.

Paul was furious about the bill. He demanded, "What are we doing with this bill? We are registering all the American people! And you want to register the criminals, and the thugs, and the terrorists! But why does a terrorist need a driver's license? He can just steal a car… So you are registering all the American people because you are looking for a terrorist and all the terrorists are going to do is avoid the law!"

A second immigration bill, the Border Protection, Anti-terrorism and Illegal Immigration Control Act (HR 4437), entered the House floor during 2005. If passed, the bill would enable the construction of a 700-mile fence on the US-Mexican border. It would also increase penalties for both human trafficking and employing illegal immigrants. Although Paul never took a stance on this bill on the floor, he voted for it on December 16, when it passed by a margin of 239 to 182.

Despite criticism from many libertarians, Paul stood firm on his decision regarding the Mexican border fence. During his 71st birthday in August 2006, he invited Chris Simcox, the cofounder of another volunteer border patrol group, the Minuteman Civil Defense Corps, to an event. At the fundraising barbeque Paul gave an interview where he stated that securing the fence was not enough and that it needed to be accompanied by further immigration reform.

The same year, a more specific bill on the border fence entered Congress; the Secure Fence Act of 2006 (HR 6061). This bill resembled the Border Protection bill of 2005, but instead of dealing with a broad number of immigration related subjects, the Secure Fence Act only dealt with the 700-mile long triple layered border fence and its future surveillance. House Republicans supported the bill almost unanimously while only a third of Democrats favored it.

Paul addressing Minuteman Project leaders

As with the Border Security bill, Paul did not take a stance on the House floor. Instead, he voted for the bill, which passed with 283 votes for and 138 against on September 14, 2006. Paul said he favored the bill because "[w]hile the American people are demanding real immigration reform, many in Washington lack the political will to do what is required. That's why I've joined my colleagues in the House Immigration Reform caucus in demanding legislation this year that focuses on securing physical control of our borders while rejecting amnesty in any form. Congress has taken notice, and took an important first step last week by passing the Secure Fence Act of 2006—legislation that provides physical security by lengthening border walls and creating a virtual border fence that extends thousands of miles."

In total, the 109th Congress passed five immigration bills, but Paul felt it did not truly address the problem of illegal immigration. "With the November elections looming, politics is taking priority over sensible policy," he wrote. "It appears congressional leaders have no intention of addressing the issue of illegal immigration this year, preferring not to tackle such a thorny problem for fear of angering voters one way or another."

In his view, Congress was merely delaying true immigration reform, leaving the issue for the next Congress to solve. "The American people want something done about illegal immigration now—not next year. All sides in the immigration debate agree that the current, 'Don't ask, don't tell,' policy cannot continue."

In order to solve the immigration problem, Paul suggested six steps:

1. Physically secure the borders and coastlines.
2. Enforce visa rules on those already in the country.
3. Reject amnesty.
4. End welfare-state incentives for illegals.
5. End birthright citizenship.
6. Improve the legal immigration process.

Philosophically, he wanted to abandon the entire welfare state and have almost no immigration restrictions. Because political consensus did not allow this, his plan included a transition period, consisting of gradually reducing dependency on welfare benefits, while the size and scope of the welfare state was incrementally reduced. Until this occurred, he believed immigration must be restricted.

Paul's knees held strong for his final speech of the 109th congress on September 7, 2006. In his address, he restated his political beliefs, emphasizing that government solutions did not work and that congress had, for the past 50 years, mostly caused havoc in the economy and decreased American liberties. In order to restore a sound economy and American freedom, he suggested that politicians should resist PACs and lobbyists, while seeking guidance from the constitution.

Chapter 20

Republicans in the 2006 congressional election knew they were in for a difficult fight when the tide turned on popular national sentiment towards the Iraq war. Ron Paul had been opposed to the war from the start, so he would likely remain popular in November for the general election. However, he had taken the position of opposing a Republican president's war, making him potentially vulnerable among Republicans in the primary race—if someone decided to oppose him.

Sure enough, opposition came. Paul's opponent in the primary race was Cynthia Sinatra, a 52-year-old international attorney and ex-wife of Frank Sinatra Jr., the son of the legendary entertainer. Frank even campaigned at her side.

Frank Sinatra Jr. and Cynthia Sinatra

Sinatra accused Paul of not supporting his president in war. She told voters, "I support the president and Dr. Paul doesn't. [...] The world looks to us as a shining example for democracy." The tactic failed to win her much support. Paul won the 14th district with nearly 80 percent of the vote, proving, yet again, that he seemed inoculated against national party sentiments.

In the general election held in November, Congressman Paul would face Democrat Shane Sklar, a 30-year-old conservative

Democrat and former Executive Director for the Independent Cattlemen's Association of Texas. In 1999-2000 he worked for Democratic Congressman Chet Edwards, but had never run for elected office himself.

Paul's Democratic opponent Shane Sklar

A poll of 500 voters in the 14th District, conducted in April 2006 by the Sklar campaign, indicated that Paul was out of step with his constituents and they were ready for a change. The poll also indicated that when voters were exposed to his voting record, and Shane Sklar's profile, they preferred Sklar 54% over Paul's 30% (with 16% undecided). However, Paul's name recognition was 88% in his district compared to Sklar's 25%.

The Sklar campaign moved forward with a strategy to emphasize Paul's libertarian label, which many voters perceived as negative, and Paul's voting record, which Sklar said was evidence that he was promoting his own personal ideological agenda over bringing federal money and jobs back to the 14th District.

As the elections drew near, Paul's dedicated base of support did not fail. With 97% of his donations coming from individuals, he out-raised Sklar $1.2 million to $600,000. He went on to win the general election, defeating Sklar by a 20% margin.

A perfect storm was gathering force in American politics that made a presidential bid seem more plausible than ever. Sitting President George W. Bush was finishing his second term and Vice President Cheney had no intention of entering the race. For the first time since 1952, there would be no incumbent president or vice-president to run against in the general election. For Paul, from a strategic standpoint, it was either now or never.

On November 22, 2006, 15 days after Paul's congressional victory, Chris Elam, a former Washington staff intern for Paul, registered the domain name RonPaul2008.com. Although no announcement had been made, it was a clear indication that Paul was mulling over a second presidential run. News that he was exploring a run for president leaked out across the Internet.

In the meantime, Paul returned to Congress. He began his tenth term in the same way he ended his ninth term—by vocally opposing the war in Iraq. In January 2007 alone, he addressed the House three separate times concerning his country's foreign policy. Though the war had already dragged on for 45 months, he was still one of the few Republican voices against foreign policy in Iraq.

The Democratic Party had managed to capture a majority in the House of Representatives, primarily due to the growing anti-war sentiment in America. However, rather than discussing ways to scale back the war, talk immediately began of the need for a surge of an additional twenty thousand troops and one hundred billion dollars. Paul was convinced that members of the CFR had more influence on foreign policy than elected officials.

It was becoming apparent that neither the current administration, nor the newly elected Democratic majority in the House, intended to do anything other than escalate the existing war and perhaps embroil the United States in a new war with Iran. "Rumors are flying about when, not if, Iran will be bombed by either Israel or the US, possibly with nuclear weapons," he warned. "Our CIA says Iran is ten years away from producing a nuclear bomb and has no delivery system, but this does not impede our plans to keep 'everything on the table' when dealing with Iran."

Paul's anti-war stance promised to make him stand out among his fellow Republicans. With no presumptive front-runner on the Republican side, a crowded field of candidates began forming exploratory committees. By the end of January 2007, a total of ten candidates would announce their intention to run for the Republican nomination. Though he was in his tenth term as a Congressman, the GOP had never fully embraced Paul as a Republican. Some were openly antagonistic and most considered him an outsider.

At 71 years of age, he had no interest in running as a protest candidate or to simply inject often neglected issues into the debate. If he was going to do this, he would be in it to win. On January 10, after serious consideration with his family, Paul decided to go for it.

On January 11, the Associated Press broke a story with a short article titled 'Texas Congressman Seeks Presidency.' In just over 200 words, it explained that Paul had filed papers to form an exploratory committee for a presidential run.

He had the full support of his family, and the first official member of the campaign team was his son, Rand. Like his father, he was a physician, and would speak on Paul's behalf numerous times during the course of the campaign.

Paul recruited Kent Snyder as the chairman of the exploratory committee. Snyder grew up in Kansas and later attended Golden Gate University in San Francisco, where he pursued an undergraduate degree in political science. The openly gay political operative had been a longtime fan of Paul, having researched his congressional career during his graduate level studies.

The two first met in 1987 when Snyder, a 28-year old martial arts master with a black belt in Kajukenbo, was working on Paul's Libertarian presidential campaign. Paul described Snyder as a "gentle man who carried himself with quiet dignity." From that time forward, they worked together on many liberty-oriented projects. He was the executive director of the Liberty Committee, a caucus of liberty-minded US House Representatives. Snyder saw his involvement in the Liberty Committee as a way to "ensure that the Constitution is seen neither as a dead letter, nor living document but rather the law of the land to be respected and obeyed."

In 1995, Snyder left a position in telecommunications managing the San Francisco office of United Communications in order to serve as a congressional staff member for Paul when he returned to Congress.

In 2006, Snyder was integral in convincing Paul to run for president as a Republican. "It was Kent, more than anyone else, who urged me to run for president," he said. Snyder, 49 at the time, stepped into the role of chairman of the presidential campaign.

As they constructed their campaign strategy, the election team began to understand the difficulty of their task. "There's no question that it's an uphill battle, and that Dr. Paul is an underdog," Snyder said. "But we think it's well worth doing and we'll let the voters decide."

As further evidence of the uphill nature of the campaign, a CNN opinion poll on February 2007 indicated that Paul had the lowest name recognition of any Republican candidate who would ultimately seek the nomination. In order to help overcome this obstacle, Jesse Benton was tapped as the Communications Director. At 29 years of age, Benton was a self-described "conservative Republican hack" prior to his involvement in Paul's Presidential campaign. He was an economics major in college, and afterward worked for a number of prominent conservative groups, including Americans for Tax Reform and the American Conservative Union. He eventually became disillusioned when the rhetoric of limited government and personal liberty was not always backed up with real action. "I got to play with some big boys on the insider conservative movement and got to see how that works, and how, unfortunately, a lot of Beltway conservatives don't practice what they preach," he said.

Benton used his political experience to start a private communications firm, with the Paul campaign becoming his main client. "I'd been an admirer of Paul for many years," he said. "They needed some press work getting off the ground when they were just a two-person operation." He would become the third staff member of Paul's formal campaign team.

To succeed in his campaign, Paul would have to win over different voting blocs within registered Republicans—those who can vote in the primaries. The general public at large was immaterial to winning the primary campaign because all votes came from the GOP members only. Snyder would need to identify the major Republican groups and then begin an assault to win them to Paul's side. A well-coordinated campaign would involve a constant process of high-profile attacks, measuring the effects through polls and focus groups, and then re-planning another assault on that target group, much as Karl Rove had done years earlier for George W. Bush.

Jesse Benton with future wife Valori Paul (Ron Paul's granddaughter)

Snyder knew that if they were to campaign against men with more name recognition and more resources, he would need to devise a radically different campaign strategy. He remarked, "This is going to be a grassroots American campaign. For us, it's either going to happen at the grassroots level or it's not."

This grassroots campaign resulted in some unorthodox tactics. For example, Snyder often coordinated campaign activities with local groups around the country using video conferencing over the Internet. The meetings required little money, yet helped to build a solid core of insiders within each state.

Snyder set up a simple exploratory committee website at RonPaul2008.com. To his surprise, beginning with his dedicated base in Texas, people responded. In a few short weeks, people from all over the country—the liberty-minded remnant in America—began sending thousands of dollars through the campaign website. In just over a month's time, the exploratory committee had gathered over $500,000 with very little effort.

Paul formally announced his presidential bid on March 12, 2007, on C-SPAN's *Washington Journal*. Though he had been reluctant to run again for president, it was never because he doubted the strength of his message. He believed that the message was good and that it could unite people across the nation.

However, he was initially unsure that he was the right candidate to deliver the message. "Ron is the type of candidate who needs more than a thirty-second sound bite to be able to communicate his message," recalled Benton.

It was also difficult to judge the size of his supporters nationally. Paul wondered if this remnant of freedom-minded voters, no matter how small, would rally around him.

Though he ran as a Libertarian in the 1988 Presidential race, he was adamant from the beginning that he had no intention of running in a third party. Not only were the ballot access laws biased against third parties, he believed, but there would be no chance of getting the necessary media attention or a spot in any of the major debates. Paul vowed he would only run as a Republican—the party he had belonged to for the greater part of 30 years.

The revolution was about to begin.

Chapter 21

A few weeks after Ron Paul announced his exploratory committee, he gave an online audio interview about the impact the Internet would have on the 2008 presidential race. At the time, Hillary Clinton seemed like the presumptive Democratic nominee. He predicted, "This is not a contest between Ron Paul and Hillary Clinton so much as it is a real challenge between the people who get their information from the Internet in a quiet sort of way versus the major networks."

Paul was already anticipating the battle that would take place between the old media and the new. "The numbers of people out there who are sick and tired of what they're getting are strong enough that we can have a real impact and be very competitive," he said.

But in order for the campaign to be effective, he knew it would have to ignite at the grassroots level. "We live in a new and modern age and nobody has truly measured this. I think Howard Dean got around the edges two years ago and did pretty well ... but the technology continues to improve. The ability to reach millions of people at a very low cost is very intriguing."

Dean's 2004 run for president had set the prior standard for grassroots activism and Internet organization. But greatly improved technologies—including many that didn't exist during Dean's run—would catapult Paul's campaign to an entirely new level. Technologies such as YouTube and MySpace (which, in 2007, was larger than Facebook) allowed average people to participate in the national debate in ways that were impossible during the previous campaign season.

Early in his campaign, Paul was just as likely to be excluded by Internet media as by mainstream media. In March, he was excluded from a Pajamas Media website poll because he was reportedly polling at less than one percent. After a flurry of e-mails from his supporters, the website relented and included Paul, who quickly rose to the top of the online poll. This resulted in accusations that his supporters were "spamming" comment sections and stacking online polls.

In mid-March, the campaign switched its simple exploratory committee site at RonPaul2008.com to a new design. However, the new site was widely panned by Paul's Internet savvy supporters as being old fashioned and unprofessional in appearance. There was no way for supporters to interact with one another, no forums, no chat rooms, and no way for bloggers to communicate with the world. The extent of interaction was the ability to send email to campaign headquarters. Information about the campaign was left largely to an eclectic collection of independent blogs and websites that regularly posted Paul's writings.

This was in sharp contrast to Howard Dean's 2004 campaign website, which hosted all such features. An immediate redesign began. Paul's in-house team formed a unique vision appropriate to his philosophy. Rather than mimic Dean's strategy, the new website decentralized the most vital functions. The official blog was kept at Typepad, videos were hosted on YouTube, and the calendar was kept on Eventful.com.

Supporters were encouraged to use social news sites like Digg and Reddit to popularize Paul-related news items, and unofficial events began popping up on Meetup. The campaign immediately recognized the power of this new breed of Internet site. "Digg is real cool," commented Jesse Benton. "I wouldn't say it's a central nerve but it's part of our strategy."

At the time, it seemed odd for an official campaign to rely so heavily on third-party tools. In retrospect, the decision was made from necessity—the campaign had little money at the time. But it was also an extraordinary step that demonstrated just how frugal a campaign for president could be. Most importantly, it empowered supporters to promote his candidacy in the free market of ideas.

The only site at the time dedicated exclusively to Paul's presidential bid was the DailyPaul.com, a site created by blogger Michael Nystrom ten days after Paul filed his election papers. In keeping with the Internet's freewheeling nature, it was started without the knowledge or express permission of the campaign. Paul's eldest grandson, Matthew Pyeatt, credits the site as "serving a vital function in the early months of the campaign, as it was the only central gathering place for Ron Paul supporters to communicate with one another."

While small battles raged on the Internet, the campaign began trying to attract media attention. In early 2007, Benton gave an optimistic interview. "I don't think we are being completely bypassed," he said. "The mainstream media has been covering us more and more." Benton commented on the amount of coverage Paul received, saying, "I think it's legitimate that a candidate has to make some buzz before the mainstream media starts to pay attention." To succeed, he would have to make some buzz. But when the buzz happened, would the media respond?

In the years leading up to his campaign, Paul had occasionally appeared as a guest commentator on news programs and talk shows, but he was not a household name. A few memorable exchanges on national television would soon change that.

Paul initially received national exposure in late March 2007, when he was invited as a guest on *Real Time with Bill Maher*, a political talk show on HBO. Paul gave a five-minute interview via satellite.

Maher had on previous occasions described himself as a libertarian. However, his support for gun control, regulation of business, and opposition to home schooling brought that claim into question. "I've always thought I was a libertarian but I'm Chairman Mao compared to you," Maher began his interview. "You think we should get rid of the CIA! ... I would feel naked without the CIA."

The skeptical host took special issue with Paul's belief that the Civil War was unnecessary and could have been avoided. Paul had earlier endorsed the 2002 book, *The Real Lincoln*. The thesis of the book was that the Civil War was fought to prevent the southern states from declaring independence from the Union—not primarily to eliminate slavery.

"I've read that you said that you don't think we should have fought the Civil War!" said Maher.

Paul replied, "I think there would have been a better way. Every other major country of the world was able to get rid of slavery without a civil war. The Civil War wasn't fought over slavery. The Civil War was fought over unifying and making a strong, centralized state."

"What about global warming? Are you on the page that there is such a thing as global warming?" Maher asked.

"Yeah, I think it's been around for a long time, and it's probably going to be here for a while longer," began Paul, referring to rises in temperature that began largely before automobiles came into use. "I don't think everybody knows everything about global warming, because you have reputable scientists on both sides of that argument..."

Stunning his audience, Maher cut in and yelled, "No you don't!"

Unperturbed, Paul changed tactics and explained his view that oil companies are essentially subsidized by the government via wars in the Middle East to protect their oil properties. The response garnered an enthusiastic round of applause. The obviously bothered host prodded back, "But still against the Civil War."

By early spring of 2007, old media coverage of the campaign

remained sparse as online activity continued to grow. Supporters began exploiting the Internet to share their skills and ideas about how to promote Paul in the physical world. Posters and stickers in support of the campaign were designed, uploaded and made freely available for anyone to download, print and distribute. Among the most popular was "Google Ron Paul."

While not receiving the same level of coverage on television or in print as his competitors, the Ron Paul Revolution (as it came to be known) developed through the unregulated freedom of the Internet. The campaign clearly demonstrated the battle between the vested powers of the traditional old media and the rising power of Internet-based media.

Although he did not have a detailed technical understanding of the Internet, Paul grasped the importance of keeping the Internet free from government interference. "He is really interested in the Internet," said Benton in 2007. "He recognizes the power of the Internet and the need to make sure that the Internet is not regulated and not interfered with by government because it is one of the last true vehicles of liberty."

The central issues that Paul championed during his years in Congress—freedom, liberty and limited government regulation—were central to the Internet's explosive growth. Likewise, Paul never voted to regulate the Internet, a major contributing factor to his solid Internet following. When Paul went looking for a base online, he found it already there waiting for him.

Throughout his tenth term, he would oppose any attempt by the Federal government to regulate the Internet. "The Internet is a powerful tool, and any censorship of Internet activity sets a dangerous precedent," he explained to his House colleagues. "Many Americans rely on the Internet for activities as varied as watching basketball games, keeping up on international news broadcasts, or buying food and clothing. In the last few years we have seen ominous signs of the federal government's desire to control the

Internet. The ostensible reasons are to protect Americans from sex offenders, terrorists, and the evils of gambling, but once the door is open to government intrusion, there is no telling what legitimate activity, especially political activity, might fall afoul of government authorities."

He opposed one such bill, HR 2046, which was introduced April 27, 2007 by House Democrat Barney Frank to control Internet gambling. Paul believed the bill violated basic freedoms, saying, "The ban on Internet gambling infringes upon two freedoms that are important to many Americans: the ability to do with their money as they see fit, and the freedom from government interference with the Internet."

In late April, something happened that could have only taken place in the Internet era: the first ever interview of a presidential candidate from a college dorm room. It was conducted by James Kotecki and posted to YouTube, where it received hundreds of thousands of views. There was no capital investment required from the undergraduate. He used his computer, a web cam and an agreeable candidate. It was astonishing that an enterprising college student could so easily pull off an interview with a national politician.

In May, Ron Paul Forums debuted. It was the brainchild of Josh Lowry, a professional realtor. The website would go on to have a major impact on the campaign, allowing users to discuss strategies, organize campaign activities, and inform people of upcoming events.

Along with Daily Paul, Ron Paul Forums also helped to promote news articles to the front page of social news sites like Digg and Reddit. These websites allowed users to vote for news stories. If a story became popular enough, it was promoted to the front page. The large numbers of Paul supporters resulted in dozens of front page stories receiving millions of viewers.

On May 15, Paul was in Columbia, South Carolina for the Fox News debate at the Koger Center for the Arts. The concert hall was packed to capacity with over 2000 people, with many more outside. Paul gave a performance that differentiated him from the other nine candidates on stage. His positions—ending the war, abolishing the IRS, questioning the fundamental role of government, and giving possibly the first explanation of the inflation tax that many people had ever heard—were easy for the mainstream media to dismiss.

At the debate, he was asked whether he trusts the mainstream media. "Some of them," he replied. "But I trust the Internet a lot more. I trust the freedom of expression, and that is why we should never interfere with the Internet."

When asked which departments Paul would eliminate from the federal government, he answered that he would start with the Department of Education, Department of Energy, and Department of Homeland Security. He also pointed out that President George W. Bush ran on a platform of non-intervention eight years earlier, and in the interim had reversed that policy.

2008 Republican Presidential Candidates at the Fox News debate

A tense moment occurred when a Fox News moderator asked Paul if he was suggesting the United States invited the attacks on

9/11. Paul answered that the terrorists attacked because the United States bombed Iraq for the previous 10 years and set up military bases on Middle Eastern soil. He added, "If China was doing the same thing to us, how would we feel?"

An infuriated Rudy Giuliani jumped in and called it "an extraordinary statement" and "absurd", receiving riotous and sustained applause from the audience. Giuliani then asked Paul to withdraw his statement.

It was the most electric moment of the debate, with the audience attention fixed on the two candidates. Paul later described it as a "lonely moment." Carefully, he explained the CIA findings and gave a succinct description of the concept of "blowback." "If we think we can do what we want around the world and not incite hatred, then we have a problem. They don't come here to attack us because we are rich and free, they attack us because we are over there."

To mainstream analysts of Republican politics, this seemed to be the end of Ron Paul as a viable candidate. And yet that night, new members to his Meetup groups spiked, as donations and attention began pouring in. The exchange cemented his reputation as the maverick in the race, stealing the mantle from John McCain. That week, Maher seemed to find Paul more interesting. "I watched the Republican debate, and I saw this guy Ron Paul. He's my new hero," he said.

This first debate performance caught the attention of many who had never heard of Ron Paul. Unfortunately for the campaign, post-debate news coverage all but ignored him—standard treatment for candidates with low polling numbers.

The mainstream media replayed none of his sound-bites, instead choosing to focus its attention on the candidates they already favored. *The New York Times* article covering the debate said nothing of Paul other than to mention that he was in attendance. When columnist Paul Krugman wrote about the debate, he stated that John McCain was the only candidate opposed to torture.

By necessity, those looking for more information turned to the Internet. But even the ABC News sponsored post-debate poll excluded Paul. After many vehement email complaints by supporters, he was finally added and handily won the online poll, in addition to those at MSNBC and C-SPAN.

The war between the old media and the new was on. Within hours after the debate had finished, someone had edited footage into a Ron Paul highlights reel and uploaded it to YouTube. Internet-based discussion picked up dramatically.

Paul would need money and registered Republican supporters in order to have a genuine chance of winning the Republican nomination. With this end in mind, he held one of his first significant fundraising events in Austin, Texas on May 19, 2007. There he delivered a speech that set the tone for the rest of the campaign. Unlike most presidential candidates, he just walked up to the podium without notes or a teleprompter. His message stayed the same regardless of the audience, and it had been one he had given for years, to empty House chambers, to small clutches of supporters, and to local Texan voters. It was a message based on three key issues: foreign policy, economic policy, and personal liberty.

From the beginning of the campaign, issues of a weak dollar and the possibility of a recession were starting to make headlines as the sub-prime mortgage crisis Paul had predicted began to surface. Having built his reputation over the previous thirty years as a proponent of free markets and sound money, he used his public speaking engagements to educate the American public on these and other economic issues. "Most Americans believe in the free enterprise system," he said. "The real big welfare in the system that we have goes to the military industrial complex and the big banks."

It was soon apparent from his rallies that he was drawing in crowds from across the political spectrum, making him somewhat of a unifying candidate. His supporters came from different political affiliations: there were Independents, Libertarians, Democrats, and "even a few Republicans," as he often teased.

His broad appeal did not happen by chance. "The art of politics is to bring people together, not to be divisive," he observed. "You have to bring coalitions together." While other candidates and political parties often exacerbated the differences between groups of people, or pandered to specific interest groups, Paul chose instead to address his audiences as individuals. He told them, "Personal liberty is not a special interest."

Although he tried to bring people together, others disdainfully noted his rising popularity. One former employee became increasingly antagonistic towards him. In May 2007, his former employee Eric Dondero announced, "I am this morning, declaring my candidacy for Congress in the GOP primaries against Ron Paul. If he does not resign his seat, and if another Republican candidate does not declare against him, I will run a balls-to-the-wall campaign for Congress in Texas [Congressional District] 14. I am the guy that got Ron Paul elected to Congress in 1996. I can and will defeat him in 2008."

The threat never materialized as another Republican ended up running against Paul in the primaries. However, Dondero actively campaigned for Paul's Republican primary opponent, Rudy Giuliani, believing that the most important position a candidate could take was a strong foreign policy with military intervention always on the table.

The earlier clash with Giuliani marked a turning point for Paul. On May 24, to capitalize on this buzz, the campaign staged an event at the Washington Press Club, a popular venue for press conferences. Paul brazenly presented Rudy Giuliani (in absentia) with a reading list of books, including the *9/11 Commission Report*. The event was intended as showmanship, but it did gain Paul coverage on major media outlets such as CNN. On the popular video website YouTube, the video received over 100,000 views within hours.

The campaign was even beginning to make ripples within the mainstream media. He was discussed on the afternoon women's talk show *The View*, on CNN, and other news shows.

On May 25, Bill Maher invited Paul back to his show for a second appearance, where he received sustained cheers and applause from the mostly liberal audience. Maher opened the interview saying, "We had you on in late March, and I think we just scratched the surface. And that's really my fault. I should have scratched it more. But after I saw you in the debate, I said, 'You know what? This is a person who I really want to talk to a lot more.' And there's so many things I want to ask you."

The second appearance allowed Paul to introduce his views on foreign policy. "I have been very supportive of what I call a non-interventionist foreign policy," he told Maher. "Mind our own business and stay out of the internal affairs of other nations." Once again, his ideas received riotous applause from the audience. It was an indication that Americans of all political stripes might be ready for libertarian ideas.

In May, more videos emerged to spread virally. They were, for the most part, clips from television or simple, homemade affairs featuring headshots of people talking into their web cameras. One featured an attractive young woman announcing, "Hi Internet! My name is Rachel and I'm a junkie—a Ron Paul junkie! It started right after the debates in South Carolina. Ron Paul just inspired me so much and said so many of the things I've been wanting to hear from a politician for so long. [...] Ever since then I'm just totally hooked." Paul had awakened a segment of the population previously turned off by politics.

By the end of May, he became the most requested candidate on Eventful.com, and had twice as many YouTube videos as all the other GOP candidates combined.

As the campaign continued, funds became available and Paul was increasingly able to promote his candidacy. Following the criticisms of his frugal official campaign site, the team was determined to get it right. This time they hired a professional design consulting group, Terra Eclipse, to redesign the site. On June 5, they re-launched the website to positive reaction from supporters.

While his improved website launched, Paul was in New York for an appearance on the *The Daily Show with John Stewart*, a politically themed show on the cable TV network Comedy Central. Before the show, Paul was met by hundreds of supporters waving placards on the sidewalk.

Stewart, who had already gained prominence as a gateway figure to youth audiences, was respectful of Paul. When asked how he would spread the ideas of liberty, he replied, "I think it's a good message, but I don't believe in spreading it with guns. We should spread it by setting a good example and get others to emulate us, but not to try to force it on other people."

His statements were warmly received. Stewart remarked, "You seem to practice what you preach and you seem to preach it consistently. Even though people might disagree with the message, they can't argue that you're a man of consistent principles."

Nine days later, on June 13, 2007, Paul was back in New York for an appearance on the Colbert Report, another Comedy Central show. Stephen Colbert hosted the show, poking fun at popular right-wing news commentators by imitating them. Paul, who had never watched the show before, seemed mostly bemused by the bluster, but didn't let it deter him from staying with his usual message (he had certainly been on programs with blustering hosts before). Colbert told him, "I usually like to come to my guests with a head full of steam either on their side or against them. I'm not sure how to feel about you, but I'm passionately ambivalent. ... You voted against the PATRIOT Act. You voted against the Iraq war. But you also hate taxes and you hate gun control. You are an enigma wrapped in a riddle nestled in a sesame seed bun of mystery."

The appearances on these three popular comedy-themed shows did much to attract a young, national audience to Paul's campaign. And those who could not immediately watch his appearances had a chance to watch them on YouTube. The campaign was gaining momentum.

Paul's Internet popularity was clearly on the rise. There were old standbys for Paul news, such as LewRockwell.com or *Reason* magazine's website. However, according to USA Daily, even mainstream websites such as *The Washington Post* and the *LA Times* began noticing a multiplier effect for every Ron Paul article they carried. "Every time one of our columnists publishes a piece that touches on the campaign of Ron Paul, traffic spikes," noted one blogger. "The number of daily visitors sometimes increases as much as 3 or 4 times more than average."

Paul's campaign appearances were another matter. Earlier in the year, he didn't know who would show up as he hosted rallies across the nation. As it turned out, his rallies attracted American youth in droves. Everywhere he went, there were throngs of young voters screaming and cheering at his speeches. On June 15, in Kansas City, the campaign booked the Uptown Theater, a small venue that resulted in supporters spilling into the aisles. He had never experienced anything like it. It was an incredible contrast to his earlier years as a congressman, and the crowds would only get bigger.

On June 28, PBS hosted a debate focusing on African-American issues, moderated by commentator Tavis Smiley. All of the major Republican candidates were invited, but only Ron Paul and Mike Huckabee accepted. Paul's forthrightness was warmly received by the audience, with polite applause throughout.

After these early debates, articles began appearing in mainstream publications and he received a smattering of televised interviews. Each time he appeared, the media made a pointed effort to make clear that he had no chance of being elected. In one particularly egregious episode during July, ABC News correspondent (and former Bill Clinton advisor) George Stephanopoulos asked Paul, "What is success to you?" "Well, to win..." was the beginning of Paul's reply. But before he could finish his sentence, Stephanopoulos declared, "That's not going to happen."

It was clear Paul did not gain his early supporters because of the mainstream media, which played only a marginal role in his popularity during the 2008 presidential primaries. As the television program *PBS Now* noted, "Ron Paul has managed to not just impress people, but change them from apathetic observers to active supporters. And he hasn't done it with hugs and handshakes or the help of the mainstream media. The Ron Paul movement was borne on the power of the Internet."

Chapter 22

For Ron Paul to have a chance in the upcoming Republican presidential primaries, donations and establishment support would be key factors to a successful campaign. But while important, money and endorsements were not the only factors for success, as an unfortunate Rudy Giuliani would later find out. In mulling his run, Paul was certain he would have support, but he doubted it would be enough to offset the wealth of his establishment opponents, who, besides small donations from grassroots supporters, could also rely on corporate supporters, national party organizations, and wealthy donors to keep their campaign coffers full—all of who would want no part of Paul's limited government politics. "When you talk dollar-wise, that is a different story," he said. "Because for those individuals, groups and companies that have a special interest—the military industrial complex and other organizations; the Haliburtons of the world—this is high stakes politics."

After Howard Dean's 2004 campaign, a new strategy for political fundraising was beginning to take shape. Improvements in communications technology, along with the national nature of presidential politics, would allow the true power of a large (if spread out) grassroots base to emerge. With this new strategy, if enough people willing to give small donations were effectively harnessed, their total contributions could begin to match or even exceed traditional donors.

Owing as much to necessity as originality, the Paul campaign became an early adopter of this strategy. In August, the campaign held its first effort to harness the fundraising power of Paul's regional support. It held a Meetup contest to see which group could raise the most money for the campaign. The winner would bring Ron Paul to their region. Competition was spirited, with the Philadelphia Meetup ultimately winning. As promised, Paul arrived to stage a rally on Independence Mall—with a tent of live-bloggers next to the stage in lieu of media. This was just one experimental fundraising strategy, but his greatest successes lie ahead.

For the August 11, 2007 Iowa Straw Poll, Paul's grassroots supporters organized an "adopt-an-Iowan" program to help pay for tickets so that locals could vote in the straw poll. Supporters organized a full-page ad in the *Ames Tribune*. Drafts of the ad, which featured a bust of Paul made up by a mosaic of supporters' faces, were posted online at Ron Paul Forums, critiqued, and improved through several iterations. It was group collaboration on a massive scale. Supporters across the country sent in money to pay for the advertisement. The initiative helped Paul place fifth at the polls with 9.1%, compared to winner Mitt Romney's 31.6%.

During the September 5 Fox News debate in Durham, North Carolina, Paul fielded a follow-up question on his foreign policy views when moderator Chris Wallace (son of *60 Minutes* reporter Mike Wallace) presented him with a partisan question. "So, Congressman Paul," he began, "you're basically saying that we should take our marching orders from al Qaida? If they want us off the Arabian Peninsula, we should leave?"

Paul rumbled back, "No! I'm saying we should take our marching orders from the Constitution! We should not go to war without a declaration. We should not go to war when it's an aggressive war. This is an aggressive invasion. We've committed the invasion and it's illegal under international law. That's where I take my marching orders, not from any enemy." In his previous exchange on the subject, he was almost booed out of the auditorium. This time he was met with a more balanced audience response.

After the debate, Paul won a poll conducted by text message by Fox News, but newscasters largely ignored the win, claiming it was the result of multiple entries from a few ardent supporters.

On September 10, he made an appearance on *The O'Reilly Factor*, a political commentary show on Fox News hosted by Bill O'Reilly. The two sparred throughout the interview, making for a lively debate. Both O'Reilly and Paul appeared flustered at times, with O'Reilly interrupting at least twice.

After the appearance, the host received hundreds letters from Paul supporters complaining about the interruptions. He responded by saying that if he feels the interviewee is dodging his questions, he cuts them off. "He started to give a history lesson we didn't have time for," said O'Reilly. "I have a six minute window. If Ron Paul wants to give me a 20 minute history lesson on the Middle East, I can't let him."

The official campaign's first real breakthrough in harnessing the fundraising power of the online community came on September 17—Constitution Day. In order to celebrate the writing of the constitution in 1787, the campaign set a goal to secure 1,787 donations by Friday, September 21. Organizers set up an online counter on the official site to show the number of donations that had been made, and it was updated each time a new one came in. This first fundraising campaign was a modest success, with the number of donations exceeding the goal by several hundred.

Emboldened, the campaign set an ambitious goal to raise $500,000 in the final week of the third quarter. A new real-time counter was added to the campaign website to record donations as they poured in. The $500,000 level was achieved so quickly—within days—that the campaign upped the target to one million dollars, which also was easily achieved.

As a result of this, the mainstream media focused its curiosity on his Internet support. By September, *Time* magazine called him the top Internet candidate—Republican or Democrat—based on traffic flowing to his site. It seemed like the Ron Paul Revolution, as supporters called it, should have warranted a good deal of media attention. He had energized the new left, the old right, and the disaffected middle, as well as harnessed the power of new technologies in a way other campaigns had barely grasped yet.

However, aside from programs that catered to younger audiences, primetime network programming—*Nightline*, *60 Minutes*—did not see a story in Paul worthy of consistent coverage. Between August 2006 and August 2007, Paul was mentioned 4,695 times on television news and cable shows—13 times per day. During the same period, fellow Republican contender John McCain was mentioned 95,005 times.

Reason Magazine editor David Weigel summarized the media's view of Paul. "The press has storylines," he explained. "The storyline for McCain is that he's a maverick who speaks the truth. The storyline for Obama is that he is God's only son sent to sacrifice himself for us, and the storyline for Hillary Clinton is that she is this terrible Glen Close in *Fatal Attraction* shrew. The storyline for Ron Paul is what a nice old, old man. He's raising lots of money but he doesn't matter. So the questions were never very respectful."

During the October 9, 2007 CNBC/Wall Street Journal debate in Dearborn, Michigan, opponent Mitt Romney answered moderator Chris Mathews' question on whether Congressional authorization is needed for an attack on Iran. Romney said, "You sit down with your attorneys and [they] tell you what you have to do." This generated a memorable Paul rebuttal. "This idea of going and talking to attorneys totally baffles me. Why don't we just open up the Constitution and read it? You're not allowed to go to war without a declaration of war." More applause.

When it came time for the Republican Jewish Coalition candidate's forum on October 16, 2007, Paul was not invited to attend.

According to the *Jewish Telegraph Agency*, he was excluded due to his "record of consistently voting against assistance to Israel and his criticisms of the pro-Israel lobby." Rudy Giuliani, Mitt Romney, Fred Thompson, John McCain, Sam Brownback, and Mike Huckabee were all invited, though Huckabee declined the invitation. It was almost a mirror image of the Tavis Smiley debate hosted earlier by PBS.

Building on its previous fundraising success, the campaign set an even more ambitious target of $12 million for the new quarter. A revised counter was placed on the website. This was the campaign's true innovation—real time, open donation counting. It had never been done in a political campaign before.

In the first few weeks of October, fundraising was lagging behind the $12 million goal. Then the grassroots movement generated a new tactic. They targeted one specific day for fundraising, November 5, inspired by the recent film *V for Vendetta*.

The original concept came from Paul supporter James Sugra, who conceived of the idea and created a video that suggested 100,000 people donate $100 each for a $10 million day. The concept was first brought to the Ron Paul Forums by Trevor Lyman, an Internet entrepreneur, where it was discussed and fleshed out. Lyman produced a website, with the help of other designers across the Internet. Someone else produced promotional banners to use on other websites. A separate artist created a flash countdown clock. In a stroke of genius, someone called the fundraising day a money-bomb. News of the upcoming event spread virally across the Internet.

By October 25, Paul was enduring several attacks from the media. *The Lone Star Times*, a minor Republican-leaning newspaper from Texas, created a grim story linking Paul with racism. It reported that a Florida resident named Don Black, the owner of a white supremacist website, had contributed $500 towards the campaign. Despite these events being entirely out of Paul's hands, the story was soon picked up by major media outlets, including MSNBC, CNN, PBS and Fox News.

Several advocacy groups, such as the Anti-Defamation League, began applying pressure on Paul to return the donation. Characteristically, he did not cave to their demands. Campaign spokesman Jesse Benton explained, "If people who hold views that the candidate doesn't agree with… give to us, that's their loss."

Paul found himself seated in *The Tonight Show with Jay Leno* greenroom on October 30, anxiously awaiting an appearance in front of mainstream America. It was the largest national coverage his 2008 campaign would receive. Things looked good for Paul as he sat watching the show backstage. Every time Leno mentioned his name the audience went wild.

After Paul's genial interview, the show continued when Leno introduced the evening's musical act, the anarchist punk rock band The Sex Pistols, prefacing his introduction by telling Paul, "We have a band that is just right for you."

The Sex Pistols performed their signature song, "Anarchy in the UK", whose lyrics begin, "I am the anti-Christ..." Lead singer Johnny Rotten yelled to Paul during the song, "Hello Mr. Paul" and later "When are you getting out of Iraq, Mr. Paul?" and "Mr. Paul! Anarchy! Mr. Paul!"

Afterward, he was happy to greet the band and shake hands, even though most politicians would have shuddered at the thought of any association with the Sex Pistols for fear of scaring away half of Middle America.

Much of the mainstream focus on Paul was the result of the televised Republican debates. He participated in four major debates in the third quarter of 2007 and five in the fourth quarter. Most were hosted by major news networks such as MSNBC, CNN, and Fox News.

Overall, Paul was satisfied with his treatment in the debates. In an official campaign video, he admitted, "I think we've had a decent shake. They could have excluded us from the debates. But we never got an even amount of time." Paul's observation that he received less time than other candidates was not inaccurate. In one MSNBC debate, his opponent Mitt Romney was allotted twenty-two minutes compared to his six.

On November 5, 2007, the money-bomb organized by Trevor Lyman raised over $4.2 million, largely in online donations. Although the unofficial drive failed to achieve the stated $10 million goal, the results were staggering nonetheless—the largest amount ever by a candidate in a one-day online fundraising event until that time. But the best was yet to come.

Afterwards, he began to receive even more press coverage. The fundraising milestone created buzz for the campaign among the media and energized his supporters. Most of the commentators seemed curious how Paul did it, but as he was quick to point out he didn't do it—it was the message of freedom that was generating so much support.

Paul's Internet success soon changed his perception among his House colleagues. In an interview on *Morning Joe*, host Joe Scarborough noted, "When we were members of congress, a lot of the time you would go on the floor, you would sit alone. People treated you like you had the plague. [...] But now you say that when you walk onto the floor, you're a popular guy. Republicans surround you and they want to know about one thing: how are you raising all that money?"

Paul chuckled at the genuine truth of those words. "They do ask me about it. Democrats are interested too," he said. "But they're asking the wrong question. It isn't a technique, it's a message."

Paul's tremendous online success overshadowed the other candidates in almost every category: most MySpace friends (later surpassed by Barack Obama); most cumulative YouTube video views of any candidate; most Facebook friends (again, later surpassed by Obama), most demands by Eventful, the most popular website of any GOP candidate, and the most Meetup members. Paul had 88,576 members in 2007, while Barak Obama, the leading Democrat, had 3,643.

Perhaps looking for a way to spin a positive story into something negative, some members of the media attempted to link Paul's record fundraising day to terrorism because the money was raised on Guy Fawkes Day, a day commemorating Fawkes attempt to blow up the British parliament buildings. Furthermore, they didn't like the concept of the money-bomb because it contained the word "bomb" in it. Neither of these images sat well in the post-9/11 climate.

Paul's supporters continued to evolve their strategies throughout the remainder of 2007 in an impressive show of creativity. As big as the November 5 money-bomb was, it was merely a prelude to what the community had planned for December 16—the 234th anniversary of the Boston Tea Party. Organized again by Trevor Lyman entirely over the Internet, the Boston Tea Party was not only a fundraiser, but a day of celebratory events held across the nation.

Although the Tea Party movement did not gain national attention until 2009, Paul's grassroots volunteers were already laying the groundwork. In his book *The Tea Party Goes to Washington*, son Rand Paul reflected on the Tea Party celebration at Faneuil Hall—the historic 1742 building referred to as "the cradle of liberty"—where he was the keynote speaker. He recalls that even then, he knew "something big was happening at the grassroots of American politics. The event featured an array of constitutional scholars and limited government advocates, and we shocked the establishment on that date by helping Ron Paul set an all-time record for online fundraising by collecting over $6 million in one day. Something was definitely brewing."

A total of 58,407 donors combined to give a total of $6.04 million, topping Paul's already record-breaking one day haul of political donations in presidential primary campaign history. These two fundraisers—organized independently, online—led the campaign to raise nearly $20 million for the quarter, exceeding the original $12 million goal by over 60%. Despite his substantial media gap, Paul was proving that, on money alone, his campaign was for real.

Paul's fundraising successes resulted in a December 23 appearance on the MSNBC program *Meet the Press*. Host Tim Russert had previously worked for the respective senatorial and gubernatorial campaigns of Democrats Daniel Patrick Moynihan and Mario Cuomo. Russert was known for asking tough questions. Just two weeks earlier, he had conducted a particularly hard interview with former New York mayor Rudy Giuliani.

Now it was Paul's turn. Despite suffering from a cold at the time, he performed well early on and was able to convey his major positions on taxation and foreign policy, addressing Russert's doubts on pulling troops out of Korea and the Middle East.

One of Russert's main concerns was over Israel. He asked, "So if Iran invaded Israel, what do we do?"

Paul replied, "Well, they're not going to. That is like saying 'Iran is about to invade Mars.' I mean, they have nothing. They don't have an army or navy or air force. And the Israelis have 300 nuclear weapons. Nobody would touch them."

Russert followed up by asking, "Would you cut off all foreign aid to Israel?"

Paul replied, "Absolutely. But remember, the Arabs would get cut off, too, and the Arabs get three times as much aid altogether than Israel."

Later in the interview, regarding the reasons terrorists attacked the United States, Russert asked, "It sounds like you think that the problem is the United States, not al-Qaeda."

Paul replied, "No, it's both. … It's sort of like if you step in a snake pit and you get bit, who caused the trouble? Because you stepped in the snake pit or because snakes bite you?"

Russert then pointed out that Paul's district received almost $4 billion in federal payments, among the highest in Texas. Of this amount, Paul himself added $400 million in congressional earmarks—amendments to bills that direct funds for specific projects within a district. He had requested funds for several projects in Brazoria, a coastal district, for such things as removing a sunken ship from Freeport Harbor and money for improving the Gulf Intracoastal Waterway. Considering Paul's objection to pork barrel spending, it seemed hypocritical.

Although he was forced to admit he added earmarks for his district, Paul explained that he had never voted for earmarks. He would instead add his district's priorities to budget bills, and then vote against the bills. According to Paul, he viewed it as representing constituents who wanted some of their money back from the Federal Government, almost like a tax credit. "I vote against it, so I don't endorse the system," he said. But if Congress passed it against his wishes, he would at least see his constituents taken care of. The explanation did not sit well with the host.

Russert also brought up the Civil War. When questioned on whether Abraham Lincoln could have avoided war, Paul replied, "Absolutely. Six hundred thousand Americans died in a senseless civil war. No, he shouldn't have gone to war." Russert then made the claim that in 2008, without the Civil War "we'd still have slavery," sparking Paul to reply, "Oh, come on, Tim. [...] Every other major country in the world got rid of slavery without a civil war."

Though Paul was applying his traditional anti-war stance to the American Civil War, explaining that there would have been more constructive ways to abolish slavery without the expenditure of lives and resources made during the Civil War, his comments were taken out of context. The *Meet the Press* appearance provided fodder for other journalists who were unsympathetic to his campaign.

Days later, he appeared on *Morning Joe* on MSNBC (the eponymous Joe Scarborough was absent). Paul was introduced, "Now joining us by phone, Republican Presidential Candidate Ron Paul, who made some remarkable comments about Abraham Lincoln on Meet the Press this past Sunday."

The host immediately put him in the hot-seat. "Some of your supporters were expressing some frustration that you would suggest that Abraham Lincoln started the Civil War, and also that Abraham Lincoln went to war just to enhance and get rid of the original intent of the Republic. Would you like to publicly take this opportunity to take back those remarks?"

Paul took a breath and replied, "Well I wouldn't mind discussing them." The next seven minutes were spent in a heated debate, with Paul on the defensive.

Paul ended the debate, saying, "I did not even bring it up in the first place, but of course I'm going to respond. This idea of avoiding the catastrophic war that is going on right now because you want to re-fight a war 150 years ago that neither of us can change or deal with—this is misdirection."

Despite several conflicts with media personalities, in late 2007, Paul had developed a group of supporters who were excited to promote his candidacy. Trevor Lyman, the man behind the money-bombs, promoted the idea to fly a Ron Paul blimp over election states. It was certainly not a focused attempt to target Republican Party members, but it would be hard to miss and awaken others to Paul's message. It was big, it was bold, and, he thought, it would likely create some buzz—at least if anyone else's supporters had hatched the idea.

Predictably, the media did not respond in kind. There was very little coverage of the blimp. Paul later reflected on the campaign with his usual sense of optimism and good humor. In his half-joking words, he said, "We never cracked the mainstream media, but if we had the election on the Internet I would have won with

80% of the vote."

With the primaries rapidly approaching, the campaign was anxious to see whether this impressive show of online support would translate into votes.

Flying the Ron Paul Blimp

Chapter 23

January 2008 heralded the start of a new year and a new primary season. Ron Paul had been campaigning steadily for the past year. Despite his overwhelming Internet popularity, however, polls of registered Republicans showed that he was only enjoying 5 to 10% support from likely voters. Soon, registered Republicans would begin casting their votes.

The campaign team itself tended not to focus much on polling. Early on, the campaign's budget dictated that it had to make maximal use of its resources—polling was not a top priority. Messages that resonated with Paul's growing group of supporters didn't always appeal to tried and true Republican Party voters, and much of the strategy wasn't appealing to reliable Republicans, but rather activating new voters.

The campaign began 2007 with six paid staff members, and only later expanded when a surge of donations came in late 2007. They could not hire someone like Frank Luntz, a Republican pollster who had helped George W. Bush's campaigns in 2000 and 2004, to carefully test sound bites and speeches on voters.

Pandering to the party-base was not on Paul's agenda. As he had previously demonstrated in the Republican debates, he was willing to state his true beliefs no matter who was listening. Instead of pandering, Paul's message to the Republican Party was, as he said at the Republican debate in South Carolina, that it had "lost its way."

At the dawn of 2008, John McCain was roughly tied in national polls with Mike Huckabee. Mitt Romney enjoyed a small lead over them both, and seemed the likely front runner. The press, however, didn't seem to care much for Romney, which would be difficult for him to overcome.

The January 3 Iowa Caucuses marked the start of the delegate selection process. Just months earlier, Romney had finished with 32% at the Iowa straw poll, with Huckabee in second place at 18%. Paul had taken fifth place with 9.1% (John McCain had skipped the straw poll). But on this night, Huckabee took the lead. Many credited his surprise win to an appearance on the *Tonight Show with Jay Leno* the previous evening, in which he played guitar with the Tonight Show Band. Paul received 10% of the popular vote to McCain's 13%. Although not spectacular, the low finish for Paul was not devastating, since most people looked to New Hampshire for a better forecast.

On January 4, Paul had an affable interview with Bill Moyers on PBS. Fox News, however, was much less welcoming. The station had earlier announced they were excluding him from attending their New Hampshire forum with the other candidates, despite his virtual tie with McCain and Huckabee in recent polls. The news channel maintained that Paul was excluded because their portable studio wasn't big enough to hold six candidates.

Paul's campaign issued the statement, "Given Ron Paul's support in New Hampshire and his recent historic fundraising success, it is outrageous that Paul would be excluded. Paul has consistently polled higher in New Hampshire than some of the other candidates who have been invited." The statement was referencing the lower poll numbers of Rudy Giuliani and Fred Thompson, both of whom had been invited to the Fox debate.

The New Hampshire Republican Party sided with Paul, officially withdrawing support of the Fox News event. While he was disappointed at being excluded, he acknowledged that, as a private business, Fox News was under no obligation to include him. "I realize they have property rights and I'm not going to crash the party," he later said.

To combat the omission, the Paul campaign hurriedly organized a forum on the same night as the Fox News debate. He was able to present himself to voters in New Hampshire with a televised town hall meeting. However, the Fox News debate, which included all the other candidates, inevitably attracted more viewers. To those unaware of the controversy, it appeared as though Paul was not one of the true contenders.

Paul meeting fans prior to his Tonight Show appearance

News of the Fox snub spread to Tonight Show host Jay Leno, who had enjoyed Paul's visit months earlier. He phoned Paul on the evening of January 6 to invite him on the show the night before the New Hampshire primaries.

Before introducing Paul, Leno said, "Let me tell you why Ron Paul is here. They had this Republican debate in New Hampshire and they did not let Ron Paul in the debate. He's tied with Giuliani and he's raised more money than the other candidates recently, so there's got to be a reason why Fox did not allow him in the debate."

During the interview, an animated Leno commented on the lack of coverage about the controversy. "I saw you interviewed by Wolf Blitzer on CNN and it wasn't mentioned. I didn't see it on MSNBC or any of the other cable channels. It seems like a big story!"

Although Paul's Tonight Show appearance ultimately would not have the same effect as it had with Huckabee, who faced no exclusion from Fox, it gave him a chance to air his views on freedom to an audience of millions.

On January 8, the day of the all-important New Hampshire primaries, things got even worse when *The New Republic* magazine decided to reopen his 1996 newsletter controversy with a story titled, "Angry White Man" by self-described liberal journalist James Kirchick. Former staffer Eric Dondero was responsible for encouraging Kirchick to write the piece and feeding him much of the background materials.

The article featured a doctored photograph of Paul in a confederate uniform, complete with bars and stars tie. In the article, Kirchick cherry-picked the worst examples from thirty years of Ron Paul newsletters—ultimately only finding objectionable content in the years between 1989 and 1994, after the replacement of Ron Paul & Associates manager Nadia Hayes.

The scathing article ran with the newsletters' most politically incorrect statements. Kirchick took issue with comments such as, "blacks poured into the streets of Chicago in celebration. How to celebrate? How else? They broke the windows of stores to loot." The racially sensitive comments appeared in the early 1990s, around the time of the Los Angeles riots and the O.J. Simpson case.

The article castigated comments about Martin Luther King, such as describing King as "a comsymp [Communist sympathizer], if not an actual party member, and the man who replaced the evil of forced segregation with the evil of forced integration."

Kirchick, a contributor to *The Jerusalem Post*, was not enthusiastic about Paul's proposal to end foreign aid, especially in regards to Israel. He objected to the newsletter's labeling of Israel as "an aggressive, national socialist state."

The article criticized the tone of discussions about social issues of the day, preferring a more delicate treatment. He didn't like what he read about AIDS, race relations, welfare, or even banking criticisms. In one passage, the author took exception to the newsletter "promoting his distrust of a federally regulated monetary system utilizing paper bills." The article also took aim at Paul for appearing on the conspiracy-themed *Alex Jones Show* and for writing an article for the John Birch Society (JBS) newsletter, even though Paul himself was not a purveyor of the conspiracy theories espoused by Jones and JBS.

Paul maintained he did not write the statements in question, but took responsibility for them since they appeared in his newsletters. *New York Times* writer Christopher Caldwell accepted this explanation, "since the style diverges widely from his own." Paul, however, refused to name the staff member who was responsible for the content.

Days later, speaking with Wolf Blitzer on CNN, Paul mused about why the attacks were coming then. "As a Republican candidate I'm getting the most support from black voters and now that has to be undermined," he said. "I defend the principle of libertarianism where every individual is defended and protected because they're important as an individual, not because of the color of their skin, but because of their character."

On January 8, the day of the New Hampshire Primary, the one-two punches from Fox News and *The New Republic* made their mark. Paul finished with 7.8% of the vote and no delegates—a near tie with one-time front runner Rudy Giuliani. His numbers hadn't budged from New Hampshire polling numbers in late 2007, ending his momentum. McCain came out on top with seven delegates, Romney with four, and Huckabee with one.

On January 10, however, it appeared that the tides were turning. Fox News held a debate at the Myrtle Beach Convention Center in South Carolina (with the Ron Paul blimp flying overhead). This time, Fox allowed Paul to participate in the debate, but he declined to be interviewed by Sean Hannity and Alan Colmes afterwards. In the post-debate text poll the next day, he won with 32%, followed by Fred Thompson with 22%. Hannity, who had been chased by a mob of Paul supporters and pelted with snowballs the previous night, was understandably not won over by the poll results.

After South Carolina polling closed, Paul came in fifth place with barely 4% of the vote, but ahead of sixth place finisher Rudy Giuliani. The big winner of the evening was McCain, who won an upset victory over Huckabee, and had gained the momentum in the race.

Paul's results would improve over the next few weeks. On January 15, he placed fourth in Michigan with over 6% of the vote. Mitt Romney decisively won the state where his father was once a popular governor.

Paul had higher hopes for Nevada, a state where many people embraced libertarian beliefs, but it was expected that Romney would carry the state because of the large Mormon population. Paul finished a surprising second with almost 14% of the vote, behind Romney. Very little news coverage was given to Paul's second place finish. The same day, Fred Thompson pulled out of the race, recognizing that he would have needed to win South Carolina to continue. At that point, there were five candidates left.

In Louisiana, Paul had another second place finish, behind McCain. The Louisiana caucuses are notoriously complicated. The deadline for registration was January 10, at which time Paul appeared to be the clear front runner in Louisiana. However, the state's Republican Party decided to extend the registration deadline to January 12, perhaps in an attempt to add more voters favoring one of the candidates. Paul later commented, "We didn't get all our votes counted in Louisiana, and we believe we won that election clean." The Paul campaign decided to contest the results, but by February it was clear that McCain would be declared the official winner.

Many saw Florida as a critical state, owing to its large population and its decisive role in previous elections. Competition was fierce. Rudy Giuliani put most of his campaign funds into advertising there. The night before the Florida primaries on January 24, MSNBC held a debate at Florida Atlantic University in Boca Raton. Compared to his performances in other debates, Paul did not fare quite as well in the MSNBC debate. When given the opportunity to present Senator McCain with a question, he asked about the President's Working Group on Financial Markets—a topic with which few voters are familiar.

The next day, a text message poll by the *New York Times* gave the debate to Romney with 41% and Paul with 40%. Despite these results, McCain edged out Romney at the polls in Florida with 36% compared to Romney's 31%. Because of the winner-take-all policy in that state, McCain won all fifty-seven delegates for himself. Giuliani, who was once considered a Republican front runner, withdrew from the race after a humiliating third place finish.

It was now an open slate until February 5, a date known as "Super Tuesday." The trend among state Republican and Democratic Committees had been to shift their primaries to earlier and earlier dates, ostensibly to mitigate the hugely important impact of the first few caucuses and primaries—for example, Iowa and New Hampshire—in determining the party nominees. State parties determined dates for their primaries in late 2007, while New Hampshire's state law that mandates its primary be the first in the nation pushed the date of the New Hampshire primary back to January 8, 2008. As a result of this trend, state primaries and caucuses were happening earlier than ever before. Two dozen states would hold their primaries on Super Tuesday. Pundits believed that the results of this day would conclusively determine the nominees for both parties.

Among the Super Tuesday states, California and New York were seen as critical due to their respective sizes, and the large number of delegates they would carry in the general election.

The January 30 CNN debate in Los Angeles, held at the Reagan Library, proved an interesting prelude to Super Tuesday for several reasons. It was down to four contenders seated close together: John McCain, Mitt Romney, Mike Huckabee and Ron Paul. The random seating arrangement had placed Paul in the center with McCain. Questions came in a round-robin format, with each candidate having equal time to answer each question. The unique venue of the Reagan library, with host Nancy Reagan, included California Governor Arnold Schwarzenegger in the audience.

Two days later, on February 1, Paul was in New York City for the MTV-MySpace forum. The MTV audience was important to

Paul, because many of his enthusiastic supporters were young. The candidates present at the forum included Barack Obama, Mike Huckabee, and Hillary Clinton.

Outside, there were throngs of Paul supporters, yet inside the venue, the producer-picked audience was different. It seemed like their questions were indirectly supportive of big government and domestic and foreign interventionism, and, contrary to most appearances, Paul received little applause after his responses.

Questions ranged from how the government should subsidize birth control costs to ways of ensuring that Russia didn't use oil as a "weapon against peace and prosperity." One young man wearing a Democrat lapel pin gave Paul a well-prepared statement, laden with statistics, demonstrating that young people support Democrats more than Republicans—a statement likely meant to downplay Paul's reputation of attracting young supporters. Paul turned the question around, acknowledging that most Republicans had a well-deserved decrease in youth support because of the policies they supported, but, he added, "You should come to one of my rallies and see the youth support there."

"I can bring tens of thousands if not hundreds of thousands of young people who are interested. [...] There is a strong resistance in the Republican Party not to accept the young Ron Paul people who are willing to vote Republican."

By the end of the half-hour debate, he was visibly gaining traction. A high point came when he passionately stated, "I want to be president not because I want to run your life—I don't even know how to run your life. [...] Likewise, I don't want to run the economy ... What I want to restore is freedom and a sound currency." In the end, the MTV host prompted the audience and they gave Paul a long and enthusiastic round of applause.

In the following MySpace poll asking, "Which candidate best connects with youth voters?" Paul finished first with over 50% of the vote, followed by Barack Obama with 31%. It was an indication that Paul had won the support of young people, an unusual feat for a Republican candidate.

Super Tuesday was rapidly approaching, and the candidates had all been pushing hard to win. Back in early January 2008, the Paul campaign began running a series of televised ads in California, Alabama, Colorado, Georgia, North Dakota, Louisiana, Maine and Florida.

Just prior to Super Tuesday, a few smaller states held their contests. First were the Maine caucuses, which ended on February 3, 2008. Paul finished solidly in third place, with 18% to McCain's 21%. Mitt Romney dominated the state with over 52% of the vote.

However, the focus of political observers rested on Super Tuesday. After all the votes were cast and tallied, McCain emerged as the clear winner. In California he received 42% support, compared to Paul's 4.2%. In New York, 52% compared to 6.5%. One highlight of the day was Montana, where Paul finished with 25%, a close second to Mitt Romney.

The next day, Paul's $6.04 million one-day fundraising record was broken when the victorious Obama campaign announced they raised $6.2 million following Super-Tuesday.

A few days later, Paul released a statement to his supporters, acknowledging that there was no possibility of a brokered convention now that McCain had won. He also addressed the issue of running as a third party candidate, something many supporters desired. "I am committed to fighting for our ideas within the Republican Party, so there will be no third party run," he stated. "I am a Republican, and I will remain a Republican."

During his previous run in 1988, Paul had dreamed of being included in major debates, a dream that was realized two decades later. Although he did not garner as many votes as he had hoped for in the 2008 Republican primaries, he had presented his ideas to millions of people with national TV appearances and a strong presence on the Internet. He had amassed a politically and socially diverse group of supporters of all ages and from all walks of life—all with virtually no help from the mainstream media. He had created, nearly from scratch, a massive fundraising engine, and had built a wildly enthusiastic base that skewed young. Both were achievements that other Republican candidates only dreamed of.

Paul himself, however, chose to not channel his voters towards the party at large. Instead, he chose to stay within, but apart from, establishment Republicanism. He continued to campaign against McCain until the last. His final official appearance in the Republican Party primary campaign would prove emblematic of both his contentious relationship to his party, as well as his radical power.

The Republican Party was to hold its convention in the twin cities of Minneapolis-St. Paul, in the first week of September. There, John McCain would be officially nominated as the Republican candidate for president. Traditionally, during the convention, the also-runs in the primary contest were given speaking slots. This was a way for the party to come back together, consolidating around a nominee. It was also a way to publicize the new stars of the party, and the people who had, for the last year, been galvanizing supporters and making headlines.

When the Republican party that year released its program, Ron Paul was notably absent.

Unbowed, he immediately announced that he would organize his own convention, virtually across the street. On September 2, while Republicans were celebrating in St. Paul, his supporters would descend on Minneapolis. Dubbed the Rally for the Republic, Paul's convention would be an announcement to the world that a new breed of conservative activist had been born.

Chapter 24

After John McCain's victory, Ron Paul turned his attention towards his congressional seat. The Republican primary would be held on March 4, less than a month after Super Tuesday. In recent years, strong support in Brazoria County and his arrangement with Republican leadership had been enough to ward off potential competitors. This year, with Paul now plainly challenging the Republican establishment, it was clear someone would attempt to unseat him. Even diminishing support in his district could be used against him. He acknowledged this in a post-Super Tuesday video, saying, "If I were to lose the primary for my congressional seat, all our opponents would react with glee, and pretend it was a rejection of our ideas. I cannot and will not let that happen."

Paul would be squaring off against fellow Republican Chris Peden for his party's nomination. Peden was the mayor of Friendswood, a small city in the 14th district. As expected, neither the National Republican Party nor the Texas Republican Party endorsed Peden or helped him financially. Instead, most of Peden's funding came from personal loans to his campaign from himself and donations from family members.

Republican opponent Chris Peden

However, much of the local establishment supported Peden. Two newspapers in his district, *The Victoria Advocate* and *The Galveston County Daily News*, endorsed him.

The *Lone Star Times*, a newspaper which had been instrumental in digging up negative stories about Paul in the past, also threw its support behind Peden.

Polls showed Paul ahead of his rival 63% to 30%. In one *Lone Star Times* article days before the election titled, "Can Chris Peden beat Ron Paul," writer David Benzion cited his reasons why he thought Paul was vulnerable, adding, "In other words, I'm highly skeptical of a +33 point Paul margin." He was right, the margin was incorrect. Paul ended up carrying the district by 40.

The Democrats had no plans to contest the seat in November, knowing popularity towards Paul was overwhelming. His congressional seat was now assured and he could continue campaigning for liberty, rather than for his position in government.

Paul's reluctance to endorse McCain, even after he had secured the nomination, frustrated many Republicans, who, despite having worked to marginalize him while the primary battle was still contestable, now wanted nothing more than to add his young army of enthusiastic supporters and donors behind the nominee. According to the *Washington Times*, National Republican Congressional Committee chairman Tom Cole wanted to see Paul's supporters stay in the Republican Party and "help expand the party's ranks."

Paul, however, had no intention of changing his message to fall in line. When the Republican Party nomination race was all but over, he continued campaigning against the nominee, working to displace the neoconservative movement within the Republican Party and replace it with his own freedom movement. He said of the neoconservatives, "we don't agree with them. We agree with the Old Right, and they're the New Right, which is The Wrong."

Paul communicated his vision of the next phase of the Ron Paul Revolution as entailing nothing short of a takeover of the Republican Party. In 2008, there would be almost 40 "Ron Paul" candidates, men and women running for down-ticket races and specifically touting their "Ron Paul Republican" credentials. Some met with success, such as William Lawson, who supporters affectionately dubbed Ron Paul Jr. due to a background in medicine and physical resemblance. The rookie candidate won his Republican primary easily. However, the next battle against Democratic incumbent David Price in November would be much harder because the fourth district in North Carolina was historically Democratic. Price ended up winning with 63% of the vote.

Libertarian writer Ben Novak noted in early 2008, "Already Ron Paul supporters are becoming prominent in the Republican Party across the nation, beginning at precincts and moving up to state level. Soon they will be in positions to educate others in the party."

For many of these Paulites, one of the main motivations was to work side by side with Paul in congress to change the shape of the debate and eventually change America. Many of these campaigns were thrown together on short notice and with little strategic planning, but writers such as Novak expected the real push for Ron Paul candidates to come in the following congressional election year. He predicted, "By 2010, there will be several Ron Paul–educated members of Congress, and Ron Paul will no longer be alone. The movement is growing and will continue to grow." It was, it turns out, an accurate prediction.

The battles over the Republican Party had been previewed in the spring of 2008. During the earlier Nevada caucuses in January, Mitt Romney had won, with Ron Paul in second place and McCain in third. The Nevada Republican Party held their state convention on April 26 to elect the delegates they would send to the September Republican National Convention. The previous night, an earthquake hit Nevada, but the real seismic shift occurred at the convention.

Approximately two-thirds of the thousand-plus attendees were Paul supporters. Both Mitt Romney and Ron Paul presented speeches to rally the Republican troops, amiably chatting together before their respective appearances. However, the presence of so many Paul supporters mixed with the neoconservative leadership caused pandemonium.

The Republican leadership was represented by chairman Robert Beers. The agenda of the day was to elect 31 delegates to send to the convention. However, because the majority of the attendees were Paul supporters, they could dominate the agenda through their voting power. Their first act was to vote on a change to the Nevada Republican rules so that delegates could support who they wanted. It passed, setting up a situation in which they could vote all or most of the 31 delegates in favor of Paul.

It was a clever maneuver that would ensure they could demand some attention at the National Convention later in the year, even though the Republican Party leadership had excluded Paul. And it was all done according to party rules. Of course, it would be a nightmare for Republicans hoping to consolidate support around McCain. A band of loud, cheering, shirt wearing Paul supporters was not what they wanted to see at the September national convention. Although Paul supporters had the numbers, the Nevada Republican Party leadership had experience.

Voting began, and the early delegates were chosen for Paul. Beers hastily called a recess and went into discussions with his council. When deliberations finally resumed, Beers closed down the convention, claiming they went past the 5:00 pm time limit for their hall rental. The Ron Paul movement had been outmaneuvered.

"Our supporters started winning the votes and we were going to have the delegates," Paul later noted. "They closed down shop before the delegates were nominated, so I guess it's up in the air."

The packed room went silent for several seconds, and then chaos erupted. Shouts of "Baloney" and "Beers, you're finished" flooded the hall. Party Chairman Sue Lowden quietly snuck out the back door. Beers stuck around for a few moments to exchange words. Although he was in no immediate physical danger, he was soon escorted from the hall by concerned security guards.

As it turned out, the claim was bogus. Hall owners had allowed the convention to continue until 8:00 pm. However, after the announcement and amid the ensuing pandemonium, too many people had left in disgust. Paul spokesman Jeff Greenspan, a 21-year veteran in politics, remarked, "I've seen factions walk out, but I've never seen a party walk out."

Paul supporters attempted to continue voting, but they needed 674 attendees to meet the quorum and they were 100 short. The coup was over, at least for the moment.

The state convention was a sample of things to come for the Republican Party. Even in mid-2008, the *Washington Times* recognized that "his supporters have all but taken over at least one state Republican Party—in Montana—and some county Republican parties in Texas." The state-by-state takeover of the Republican Party that would occur over the coming years would be fraught with conflict. Paul supporters out-organized the older neoconservative party members with new technologies like Facebook, but the Republican leadership had more experience.

Paul noted he does not want to crash the party or disrupt Republican functions. He just wants to get their attention and make his point that if they want to survive, they will have to look more seriously at freedom. The beaten down Republican Party was receptive to this idea. Maryland state party Executive Director John Flynn said, "We welcome everyone to the Republican Party. [...] Two years ago we didn't even field candidates for two of these races, so the Ron Paul Republicans are really adding something."

While the campaign wound down, Paul continued giving interviews to everyone from CNN to local radio stations. Most of his interviews took place from Washington, often on the steps of the Capital Building. Behind the scenes, Paul was hard at work putting the finishing touches on a new book, *The Revolution: A Manifesto.*

It was a statement of his principles, outlining a vision for America based on the constitution. Even before release, the book dominated all other political books on Amazon.

It was released on April 30 and quickly rose to the top of Amazon.com, as well as reaching number one on the *New York Times* best seller list (non-fiction) by its second week. It was an incredible accomplishment. Normally political and celebrity books only reached the top due to massive, choreographed coverage by the major media: Larry King Live, Oprah, Good Morning America, *Time* magazine, and the New York Times itself. Paul received none of that support, yet still managed to climb his way to the top. The surprise reestablished that, although the primaries were over, he remained a powerful force in politics.

Even after Paul announced the formal end of his campaign, he stated his intention to continue the fight. "We'll make our presence felt at every level of government, where just a few people with our level of enthusiasm can make a world of difference. We'll keep an eye on Congress and lobby against legislation that threatens us," he wrote. "We'll identify and support political candidates who champion our great ideas against the empty suits the party establishments offer the public. We will be a permanent presence on the American political landscape. That I promise you."

On the same day, he launched the Campaign for Liberty in order to coordinate his supporters. His first goal was to sign up 100,000 members by September 1. He received over 35,000 members on the first day, and 38 days later the membership was over 70,000. With this new organization, he would attempt to create a permanent revolution.

Paul's enthusiasm for the new campaign was tempered by personal concern for one of his closest staff members, Kent Snyder. Tragically, on June 26, 2008, Snyder lost a two month battle with pneumonia. Paul had lost not only the man who devised the strategy for his campaign, but a close friend. He noted of his ally, "During difficult times, Kent was always a calm at the center of the storm."

Snyder's passing did not go by without controversy. Two months of lying on a hospital bed produced over $400,000 in medical costs, and Snyder was uninsured, leaving his family with the bill. While some, such as *Huffington Post*, thought it was an argument for universal healthcare, others thought it was an argument that free market medicine and insurance would have been far cheaper, with improved medicine that might have provided a cure.Paul himself received some criticism for not offering health insurance to his staff, but this was not typical for frugal campaigns. As Jesse Benton observed, "As a general practice, virtually no political campaigns offer health insurance. It's just not done. A campaign is a temporary organization that could disband at any minute."

Kent Snyder

With his presidential campaign over, it was time to assess his successes and failures. Paul himself admitted the campaign could have been better. "Some of it was because we weren't as organized as we could have been or should have been," he said.

Some of the most pointed criticisms of his campaign came from his opponents. While acknowledging that the media did not give favorable coverage to Paul, former senior aide Eric Dondero noted, "One of the reasons Ron Paul failed is because his staff ran a miserable campaign. They had more money than Huckabee but they didn't do the right things with the money, including hiring professional campaigners."

Reason magazine contributor David Weigel described how the media calculates viable candidates. "There is an eternal calculus for who has a chance and who does not have a chance," he said. "To be fair to them, some of that calculus was, 'Well, Mitt Romney has hired these guys that have won 12 elections and Ron Paul hasn't.'" If Paul wanted to impress the media in future contests, he would need seasoned campaign professionals.

July 12, 2008 Revolution March on Washington

Far from fading away, Ron Paul announced his intentions to do nothing short of revolutionize America. On July 25, 2008, the Campaign for Liberty began selling tickets to the Rally for the Republic. Tickets went on sale for $17.76 (appropriately) and half of the 10,000 available seats sold out in 12 hours. It was a good omen.

The press was already closing the book on 2008 when he told supporters, "the neocons, the warmongers, the socialists, the advocates of inflation will be hearing much more from you and me."

Chapter 25

The Rally for the Republic, on September 2, 2008, at the Target Center in Minneapolis could easily have been mistaken for a capstone event for the campaign; a celebration of a political happening before everybody moved onto other things. It might have looked like the end of a long road that, in Ron Paul's case, had begun over 30 years ago when he first entered politics.

Across the dividing line, in St. Paul, the Republican Party was busy preparing for the future with its nomination of John McCain. Commentators barely paid attention to the quixotic Paul campaign seemingly celebrating with one last hurrah. McCain was the future, whereas Paul was the past.

While the press and political pundits were focused on St. Paul, in Minneapolis, the future of American politics was taking shape.

At the roaring Target Center, more than 12,000 supporters stomped and cheered. Far from a closing ceremony, Paul had desired the event as a "celebration of the freedom movement and its supporters, as well as a call to the Republican Party to return to its roots of limited government, personal responsibility, and a protection of natural rights." He wasn't closing the door on a campaign; he was instead actively defining a new movement, one based on energetic grassroots activism in service of a limited government agenda. While McCain would emerge from the RNC as the Republican nominee for president, Paul would emerge from the Rally for the Republic as the Father of the Tea Party.

The atmosphere at the Rally was charged. Supporters waved

signs that read, "Calling the GOP Back to Its Roots!" They promised more action to come, including a refusal to stand down. This wasn't a sour-grapes gathering of sore losers, scheming to launch a third party. Instead, they were thinking strategically about how they could transform the Republican Party to reflect constitutional positions.

Paul addressing the Rally for the Republic

Introduced by Barry Goldwater, Jr., Paul took center stage and was greeted by a shower of red, white and blue confetti, and a standing ovation from the sold-out crowd. When he addressed the audience, many of whom had traveled across the nation to be there, he said "The ideas of liberty and the revolution are alive and well, and we're celebrating it here tonight!" The ensuing cheers and screams made it almost impossible for Paul to continue.

Shortly after the Rally for the Republic, the Campaign for Liberty would mobilize this grassroots army for its first initiative: Audit the Fed. Paul began writing a book to publicize his views on the Federal Reserve System. But his main attack on the Fed would occur in early 2009. For now, he began planning his strategy.

On February 19, 2009, CNBC aired Rick Santelli's famous rant from the floor of the Chicago Mercantile Exchange in which he accused the government of promoting bad behavior. He also raised the possibility of a "Chicago Tea Party." An educated and passionate grassroots base of activists was more than ready to heed the call.

Initially, Santelli's broadcast was widely credited for lighting the Tea Party fuse—which was true—but in time it became clear that Paul had laid down the fuse in the first place. Certainly, the Tea Parties of early 2009 were a distinct phenomenon from the Ron Paul campaign—even while Paul's supporters made up a significant portion of the Tea Party ranks. In fact, many of the leaders of this second wave of Tea Parties had barely even heard of Congressman Paul. It was almost as though convergent evolution within the political realm had produced two similar groups independently. However, Paul activists would ultimately provide the intellectual influence, and grassroots experience, necessary to shift the Republican Party in a Tea Party direction, and the Tea Party in a decidedly libertarian direction.

Members of the media and political establishment seemed confused by the new movement, believing it sprang out of nowhere. Only in hindsight would they recognize the unique role Paul played in its rise. *The Atlantic* magazine later observed that Paul "is not the Tea Party's founder (there isn't one), or its culturally resonant figure (that's Sarah Palin), but something more like its brain, its Marx or Madison. He has become its intellectual godfather."

Bret Baier of Fox News called Paul "the man credited by many with lighting the fire that became the Tea Party." As the Tea Party movement grew, Paul's ideas would continue to spread and demonstrate a powerful influence on the national political landscape.

With impeccable timing, Paul grabbed the media's attention just days after Santelli's broadcast. On February 26, he unleashed the most focused and sustained attack of his career against the Federal Reserve. He had been planning it for months.

Paul's first piece of artillery was introducing a defining piece of legislation into the House of Representatives: HR 1207. The Federal Reserve Transparency Act of 2009, also known as the "Audit the Fed" bill, required that, "The audit of the Board of Governors of the Federal Reserve System and the Federal reserve banks under subsection (b) shall be completed before the end of 2010." Prior to Congressman Paul's Presidential Campaign of 2008, his anti-Fed leanings were consistently dismissed by the political establishment. Auditing the Federal Reserve was an idea Paul first proposed back in 1983, and had subsequently reintroduced many times. Now, with the country approaching double-digit unemployment, increasing foreclosures, and the hints of inflation, and with the backlash against government bailouts, the ideas of a "political crank" began entering the mainstream.

The bill would require 218 votes to pass into legislation—290 for a veto-proof majority. Paul began gathering support for the bill by collecting endorsements from his congressional colleagues—a slow process which would take months. The bill was publicly opposed by Federal Reserve Chairman Ben Bernanke, Treasury Secretary Tim Geithner and others from the Obama administration.

The day after introducing the bill, on February 27, Paul attended the 2009 Conservative Political Action Conference (CPAC). The conference attracted conservative activists and elected politicians across the country. He timed his introduction of HR 1207 with CPAC in order to promote the bill.

One of the highlights of CPAC was the annual straw poll, in which attendees could vote for the politician they most wanted to lead the Republican Party in the presidential election. Previous winners included George W. Bush and Ronald Reagan. Mitt Romney had won the poll the previous two years.

CPAC was one of the first evidences that Paul's ideas were beginning to gain popularity among the Republican base. He began his address to the CPAC attendees by talking about how disconnected the politicians in Washington, DC seemed to be from the American people. Then, he commented on the state of conservatism, and the failure of the Bush administration to stand firm on the principles of limited government and fiscal responsibility. "I think in many ways the Conservative movement has had a struggle defining a conservative," he said. "We finally got the conservatives in charge. We've been struggling ever since Barry Goldwater, and Ronald Regan, and the revolution of 1994 and...[in 2000] we finally get the House and the Senate and the Presidency. And what did we do? We doubled the size of the Department of Education! I thought we were supposed to get rid of the Department of Education!"

When the results of the 2009 CPAC Straw Poll were announced, it showed the fractured condition of a movement trying to define itself. Although the results were predictably divided, few would have predicted that Paul would finish third. Earning 13 percent of the vote, he tied with 2008 Republican Vice-Presidential Candidate Sarah Palin. Though he placed behind Mitt Romney with 20 percent and then-rising-star Louisiana Governor Bobby Jindal at 14 percent, this was the highest total he had ever received at CPAC, an organization that had roundly decried Paul for his anti-war views in previous years. While the Republican base was still undecided on who should define conservatism moving forward, Paul was on the rise.

His finish was an early indicator that his anti-Fed ideas were beginning to take hold with conservatives. "That used to be a fringe idea," said Michael Tanner of the CATO Institute. "Now you see a fair amount (of legislators) demanding some sort of accountability on the part of the Fed, and there's a great deal of suspicion of Fed policy."

This struggle for the conservative movement to define itself would become a public struggle as various factions of the Tea Party movement began to take shape. Joe Wolverton, writing for *The New American*, concisely identified this in his article "Tea Party: a Brewing Movement." Wolverton said, "Given that the only thing many Tea Party adherents share is a mile-wide streak of independence, it is difficult to draw a picture of the typical Tea Partier. There are 'birthers'...and 'truthers'; there are fans of radio talk-show host Glenn Beck and fans of Ron Paul; there are libertarians and disaffected members of the two major parties; there are constitutionalists and those who feel we are Taxed Enough Already...That is to say, there is no one mold into which all Tea Party activists fit." This eclectic mix of people with different backgrounds and different beliefs prevented the movement from being easily labeled with any particular ideology.

With Paul often credited as the father of the Tea Party movement, it only made sense that his son Rand would be the Tea Party's first offspring. An ophthalmologist and Paul's middle son, Rand had participated in the December 16, 2007 Tea Party held at the historic Faneuil Hall in Boston.

In February 2009, Ron Paul's supporters began an online campaign to draft Rand to run in an effort to get rid of incumbent Kentucky Senator Jim Bunning. When asked his opinion on the matter, the congressman noted that "Should Senator Bunning decide not to run, I think Rand would make a great US Senator."

The younger Paul was intrigued by the idea. On May 14, 2009, he appeared on the Rachel Maddow Show to announce he was forming an exploratory committee. When Bunning announced on July 28 that he would not seek another term as a US Senator, it provided a unique opportunity for a Tea Party outsider to run for the office.

Rand Paul's 2010 Senate campaign would prove to be an example of being in the right place at the right time. But as was the case with his father's political career, there were hurdles, and resistance from the Republican establishment, to overcome. Paul officially announced his intention to run for US Senate in August of 2009. This was precisely the same time that the Tea Party was coming into focus as a national movement. Fueled by the heated debates over national healthcare reform, Tea Party groups began to appear all across the country. Almost overnight, the same small government rhetoric and austerity measures that Ron Paul had been prescribing for decades were suddenly in vogue. The message, which had been soundly rejected in the Republican primary less than two years ago, seemed to be catching on.

Throughout the summer, Ron Paul continued building support for his "Audit the Fed" bill. Previously, bills he introduced routinely went nowhere, but this time it was different. On June 11, Democrat Dennis Kucinich signed on to become the 218th sponsor, resulting in a majority of House members supporting the bill. By August, he had garnered 320 co-sponsors representing large numbers of Republicans as well as Democrats.

Now the bill had to get through the House Committee on Financial Services, which was chaired by Democrat Barney Frank. Frank had remained silent on the bill up until now. Then, a Democrat representative from North Carolina, Mel Watt, amended Paul's bill. In the words of Huffington Post contributor Ryan Grim, "...instead of increasing transparency, as the amendment claims to do, Watt's measure would instead make the institution more opaque." Perversely, with these new changes, the bill now gained Frank's support.

Paul teamed up with Democrat Alan Grayson to fight the Watt amendment. He told the committee, "If we allow the Watt amendment to pass, not only do we not get the Federal Reserve Transparency Act, what we end up with is more difficulty in finding out what the Federal Reserve is doing." The two created an amendment,

Paul in discussion with Barney Frank

which passed, to undo the Watt amendment. When this occurred, Frank immediately withdrew his support of the "Audit the Fed" bill.

On September 16, 2009, Paul released the book he had been working on since the previous year, *End the Fed*. In it, he tied together history, economics, philosophy, and his experiences interacting with three different Federal Reserve Chairmen, across his four decades of Congressional service. In simple language, he explained why he believed that the Federal Reserve had been "pulling the strings of the American financial system for nearly a century."

On September 29, he appeared on *The Daily Show* to promote the new book. Host John Stewart asked Paul what he thought about the sudden rise of the Tea Party, saying, "You've been rallying against this type of government intervention, and the Federal Reserve, for 30 or 35 years. Suddenly the Tea Parties arise, calling for a very similar type of thing. Do you feel like you were a cool, indie band, and then somebody came in and stole your sound, and then got super big?" Paul indicated he never intended the movement to begin and end with him. The Campaign for Liberty was all about the kind of spontaneous, grassroots activity the Tea Party embodied. He had no interest in appointing himself as their leader. Someone else would need to step forward and be embraced by the Tea Party.

When Paul's book hit the *New York Times* bestseller list on October 4, it further confirmed that the ideas he had been championing for thirty years were finally getting mainstream attention.

This became even more evident in February 2010 when he again attended the annual CPAC gathering. Mitt Romney had dominated the CPAC straw poll the previous three years, but the Tea Party had suddenly increased Paul's profile with Republicans. He would go on to post his first win at the CPAC Straw Poll—amidst a reaction of boos and catcalls from the neoconservatives in attendance.

Shortly after CPAC, he faced the primaries for his seat in the 14th district. Two years earlier he had faced one Republican challenger in the primary race. This year, he faced three. Something had changed. Tim Graney, a small business owner, held anti-tax beliefs and a distrust of too much government. John Gay, a financial planner, and Gerald Wall, a petrochemical worker, shared similar views. All three claimed allegiance to the Tea Party, reflecting the situation across much of the country. On March 2, 2010, Paul easily defeated his three opponents with over 80 percent of the vote.

Next up was Rand Paul, who faced the Kentucky senate primary election in May. Rand benefitted greatly from his father's national name recognition, his grassroots activist network, and nationwide fundraising prowess. All of these factors worked together, allowing him to amass a war chest of campaign funds that would not have been possible prior to his father's 2008 campaign—$1.138 million in the second quarter alone.

Rand soon found himself caught up in the perfect political storm. He faced four other challengers, the most prominent being Trey Grayson, the Secretary of State in Kentucky and the heir apparent favored by Kentucky's other Senator, former chair of the Republican National Senatorial Committee, and the Senate Minority Leader, Mitch McConnell. Grayson started his campaign with a substantial lead in the polls and higher name recognition. In spite of fighting an uphill battle against an establishment-backed candidate, with intra-party attacks on Rand's suitability for office, he handily won the Kentucky Republican primary on May 18 with almost 60 percent of the vote compared to 35 percent for Grayson. It was not a good year to have establishment backing. Following his defeat, Grayson considerately told his supporters, "It's time to put all differences aside and unite behind Dr. Paul. He needs our help and I for one stand ready to serve."

Immediately following his primary victory, Rand appeared on *The Rachel Maddow Show* on MSNBC. During the uncomfortable 20-minute interview that went uninterrupted even for commercial breaks, Maddow grilled Paul on comments he made about the

Civil Rights Act of 1964. Paul explained he supported 9 out of the 10 titles in the act, but disagreed with title II, which prohibited private businesses from discriminating against their customers. It was clear the left would use Paul's support of private property rights to imply he was a racist.

Following the potentially disastrous interview, Ron Paul intervened and offered his campaign manager, Jesse Benton, to replace David Adams.* To prevent any more damage, Benton canceled a scheduled appearance on *Meet the Press*—the first such cancelation in its 64-year history—and instituted a policy of only appearing on regional Kentucky media.

Things only got uglier for the rest of his campaign against Kentucky attorney general Jack Conway. Accusations began to fly that Rand had kidnapped a coed during his college years and made her smoke marijuana and worship a deity he called "Aqua Buddha." During one encounter, in which Conway questioned Paul's religion, Paul was so disgusted by the tone of the debate that he refused to shake his opponent's hand afterward. Throughout the latter part of the year, paid activists from MoveOn.org harassed Paul and his supporters along the campaign trail in an attempt to derail his momentum. It was an anxious period for the entire Paul family leading up to the election. Despite his opponent's efforts and the belief from many mainstream pundits that Paul was "too radical" to win a general election, on November 2, 2010 he emerged victorious with an impressive 11-point margin.

Incredibly, Rand Paul had achieved what his father had attempted back in 1984 with his failed senate run. In his victory speech, senator-elect Paul warned Washington that the people of Kentucky were sending him there with a message: "We've come to take our government back!"

The mid-term elections were bad news for Barack Obama and the Democrats. Normally the president's party loses on average 30

* The Republican Party of Kentucky subsequently donated $100,000 to Ron Paul's campaign.

seats in the mid-term election. This time, the Democrats lost 63 House seats and six Senate seats. It was a clear indication the Tea Party movement was having a dramatic effect on politics.

Rand Paul celebrating his Senate victory

The elder Paul had a much easier election than his son. He received massive campaign donations from the National Republican Congressional Committee and the Republican Party of Texas adding up to several hundred thousand dollars. On the same night as his son's victory, Paul received 76 percent of the vote to Democratic challenger Robert Pruett's 24 percent. He had increased his margin of victory of the previous election from 40 to 50-points, while leaving him with $1.5 million in unspent campaign contributions.

Despite the routine win, Paul now had an opportunity to add one more powerful weapon to his arsenal against the Federal Reserve. By default, he was eligible for the Chairmanship of the Financial Services Subcommittee on Domestic Monetary Policy and Technology. As Paul described it, "It's basically been a committee that's dealt with commemorative coins. I'm going to deal with monetary policy."

As Paul eluded, the subcommittee had jurisdiction over domestic monetary policy (including the functioning of domestic financial institutions, such as the Federal Reserve System) and even development of new or alternative forms of currency. It was the perfect venue for him to promote his monetary ideas.

However, he immediately met with resistance to his new appointment. In December 2010, *Bloomberg Businessweek* magazine reported that incoming Speaker of the House John Boehner was considering ways to prevent Paul from becoming chair of the subcommittee. At the very least, he wanted to restrict his authority.

In spite of this, Paul was ultimately appointed chairman of the subcommittee, which would begin sessions in January of 2011. No longer a back-bencher, he would now be running the show.

The New Year started off promising for both of the Pauls when *Time* magazine named their person of the year. Although the top spot went to the founder of Facebook, the Tea Party made the second-place cut. A clever montage of the main Tea Party leadership included both Ron and Rand Paul on a merchant ship, hurling creates of tea overboard.

On January 5, 2011, both Pauls were sworn in as representatives of their respective states. It was the first time in congressional history that a child served in the Senate while the parent simultaneously served in the House of Representatives. Comparisons to the Kennedy political family were made, calling them the "Libertarian Kennedys." With his son firmly established in the Senate until 2016, Ron Paul turned his attention to 2012.

After delivering a powerful speech at CPAC 2011 in February, Paul walked away with his second consecutive straw poll victory. Earning 30 percent of the vote, Paul topped Mitt Romney at 23 percent, with the rest of the field trailing far behind at less than 7 percent each. Compared to the mixed reception he had received the previous year, this year there was nothing but applause. Regular CPAC goers noticed that the crowds they were drawing were younger and more enthusiastic than ever before. Little by little, year by year, Paul was winning over the Republican Party.

Not everyone was happy with Paul's two consecutive victories. Mike Huckabee declined to attend in 2010 and 2011 because of Paul's influence. "CPAC has become increasingly libertarian and less Republican over the last years, one of the reasons I didn't go this year," Huckabee said. Many conservative groups began abandoning CPAC and moving to the Values Voter Summit, a more family-values and security-issues event held later in the year.

On April 21, *Time* magazine released the results of a poll for the 100 most influential people in the world. Ron Paul came in at number 14, the highest of any politician, even besting Barack Obama, who came in at number 46. The magazine described Paul as the "twelve-term Republican, a libertarian icon, an anti-war gadfly, a master of the online money bomb and a perpetual front runner in CPAC straw polls."

Rumors over whether or not Paul would run for president had been swirling around even in late 2010. Many thought he would run in his home state of Texas to join his son in the Senate. Others suspected he would hand the torch to son Rand for the upcoming election. Paul told interviewers he would only run if the economy got worse.

Curiously, other Republicans were just as reluctant to enter the race. The Republican Party was forced to postpone a scheduled May 2 GOP debate due to an absence of any declared candidates.

On May 9, 2011, Paul finally announced his decision to make his third run for the presidency. His decision to run may have been influenced by a CNN Poll released on May 5 which supported the claim that Paul had the best chance, of all likely Republican candidates, to beat Barack Obama in a 2012 showdown. Just days earlier, Osama bin Laden had been found and killed by US soldiers, resulting in a surge in popularity for the president's sagging poll numbers. The poll showed Paul trailing Obama by only seven points, besting both Mike Huckabee and Mitt Romney in hypothetical match-ups against the president.

The influence of Paul's ideas on economics and the Federal Reserve had become more pronounced since he decided to seek the Presidency again in 2012. Proof of this widespread influence within the Tea Party, and the GOP establishment itself, came during a Tea Party bus tour in June of 2011. The mission of the18-day Iowa bus tour was to make returning the United States monetary system to a gold standard a prominent election issue in 2012. The issue of sound money was almost unheard of in mainstream politics prior to Paul's 2008 presidential campaign. Now, only three years later, this tour would feature GOP presidential hopefuls Michele Bachmann, Herman Cain, Newt Gingrich, Gary Johnson, Tim Pawlenty, and Rick Santorum. The renewed interest of average Americans in gold and silver currency was almost entirely due to Paul's influence.

The same can be said for his views on foreign policy. In 2007, conservative media outlets and GOP candidates mocked his non-interventionist foreign policy during the debates. Calling for immediate withdrawal from Iraq and Afghanistan, Paul was labeled an isolationist. However, as President Obama increased the size and scope of the United States military efforts in the Middle East between 2009 and 2011, some Tea Party conservatives began to grow uneasy about the length and cost of foreign wars. This was evident at both the Fox News debate on May 5 in South Carolina and the CNN debate in New Hampshire on June 13. Unlike the debates of 2007, Paul was no longer the lone voice of dissent regarding American foreign policy. Gary Johnson echoed his position calling for immediate withdrawal. Several other candidates, including Herman Cain, expressed reservations regarding US military presence in Afghanistan and Libya.

These changes in the political landscape led Fox News contributor Juan Williams to write an article titled "The Surprising Rise of Rep. Ron Paul." He wrote, "It is becoming increasingly clear that we are living in a time when Republican politics are being shaped by a 75-year old, 12-term Texas congressman." Williams noted that the "Tea Party, which drove the GOP to claim a majority of the House in the mid-term elections, grew largely out of the ashes of [Paul's] 2008 presidential campaign, which emphasized limited government and a return to constitutional principles."

In July 2011, Paul made a surprise announcement. He would resign his seat in the House of Representatives—the seat he had held for the past eight consecutive terms—in order to focus his efforts on the upcoming presidential election. "I felt it was better that I concentrate on one election," he said. "It's about that time when I should change tactics." It was a surprising decision to many of his supporters. But at the same time, he had, in many ways, already accomplished what he had come to Washington to do—although it took him 35 years.

During the summer of 2011, with the Federal deficit out of control, President Obama's budget proposal sought to raise the debt ceiling, which would allow the US to go deeper into debt. The move was opposed by Tea Party Republicans, including Ron and Rand Paul. To their mutual disappointment, on July 31, after months of fighting, both the House and Senate voted to raise the Federal Government's debt ceiling. This resulted in the first ever downgrade of the US government's credit rating by Standard & Poor's from AAA to AA+.

The Obama administration immediately tried to blame the Tea Party for the reason for the downgrade. Ron Paul responded, "This attempt to scapegoat folks who recognize that our debt is out of control and that we must change course should not be tolerated. They are simply demanding that Washington do its job."

Rand Paul also objected, saying, "Blaming the Tea Party for America's debt crisis and downgrade is like blaming the fireman for fires. The Tea Party has been fighting for a serious solution that would rescue our finances through immediate spending cuts, spending caps and most importantly, a Balanced Budget Amendment to the Constitution."

With the focus on Tea Party issues, Paul's campaign expected to improve his poll results at the upcoming August 13 Iowa straw poll. During the previous election in 2008, he placed 5th. This time he finished in a virtual tie with Michele Bachmann, the other Tea Party candidate who previously sat alongside Paul on the same Financial Services subcommittee—4,823 for Bachmann and 4,671 for Paul.

If Paul expected a reaction by the media, he didn't get it—although Bachmann did. Paul had been polling in third place for most of the campaign, yet commentators on NBC, CBS, CNN and Fox News announced a new "top tier" of three candidates which included Mitt Romney, Michele Bachmann, and Texas Governor Rick Perry, an undeclared candidate.

On *The Daily Show*, host Stewart lampooned the bizarre reaction by the mainstream media. "This pretending Ron Paul doesn't exist for some reason has been going on for weeks," he observed. "How did libertarian Ron Paul become the 13th floor in a hotel? He is Tea Party patient zero! All that small government, grassroots business—he planted that grass. These other folks? They're just moral majorities in a tri-cornered hat. Ron Paul is the real deal."

Noting a particularly egregious comment towards Paul by a CNN host, Stewart remarked, "And even when the media does remember Ron Paul, it's only to reassure themselves how there's no need to remember Ron Paul."

The big mystery was why the media wanted to ignore him so badly. Several commentators offered up reasons. Timothy Carney of *The Washington Examiner* noted, "In part, the media ignore Paul's success at events like Ames and the Conservative Political Action Committee because they think he's almost breaking the rules by having such a dedicated following."

Paul's ability to cause embarrassment to an establishment in turmoil over the financial crisis also likely played into it. "One reason the bipartisan establishment finds Paul so obnoxious is how much the past four years have proven him correct—on the housing bubble, on the economy, on our foreign misadventures, and on our national debt," said Carney. It was painful for the mainstream media to admit that intelligent, respectable conversation could come from someone who, as they saw it, didn't occupy the political middle ground.

In an interview with Lew Dobbs, Paul was asked why he thought the media was ignoring him. He replied, "It's possible they don't understand what I'm saying, but the other possibility is that they do know what I'm saying, and they don't want the story out. Because I do challenge the status quo of the establishment when it comes to the Federal Reserve and foreign policy and a number of things you're not supposed to disagree on. Republicans and Democrats are more in agreement than most people realize. Their rhetoric is different but the policy is always the same."

Dobbs weighed in with his own theory. "I think something else is going on. I think there are some folks who think you could win. You and a number of other folks scare the dickens out of them. I think there is an establishment out there that looks a little nervous to me."

As Fox News commentator Juan Williams observed, "If you have not been paying attention, it's time to look around and realize that we are living in the political age of Rep. Ron Paul." This was a bold statement for Williams to make over a year before the 2012 elections. However, it wasn't so much a prediction about the outcome of the race, as it was an observation of a seismic shift that was already happening on the political landscape.

Brent Budowsky, writing an article for *The Hill* titled "Ron Paul has Won," echoed a similar sentiment. He said that Paul's "influence on the national debate is significant and growing, and in this sense, he is already a winner in the 2012 campaign."

Nobody was more surprised by his success in American politics than Ron Paul. When he left Congress in 1984, he believed that he would go "unnoticed and remain nameless in the pages of history." In 2010, when Paul's son, a virtual unknown from Bowling Green with no political experience, became the junior Senator from Kentucky, he knew his battle for freedom would carry on beyond his own congressional career. Joined by dozens of other newly-minted legislators who had been inspired by the elder Paul, there was now a group of politicians fighting against the entrenched establishment, backed up by an army of dedicated activists.

Paul's political campaigns went from being ignored, to being studied. Campaign strategists from across the spectrum learned from his success with decentralized activists, money bombs, and engaging American youth. His ideological campaigns have given birth to a host of new organizations dedicated to advancing his mission, from the Campaign for Liberty to the Young Americans for Liberty. Intellectually, he went from being an ignored back-bencher to best-selling author. And, as a political force, he spurred on one of the biggest political stories of the new century—the rise of the Tea Party. He went from being known as the lone nay-vote in Congress, to launching a movement that helped the GOP retake the House. And as more time passes, his influence can only grow.

Paul entered Washington in April 1976 as a soft-spoken small-town doctor just wishing to be heard. Decades later, at 75 years of age, everybody, it seemed, was listening.

Index

Symbols

A

B

H

I

N

O

P

R

S

T

U

V

W

Y